The Soul
of the
Wobblies

The Soul of the Wobblies

The I.W.W., Religion, and American Culture in the Progressive Era, 1905–1917

Donald E. Winters, Jr.

Contributions in American Studies, Number 81

Greenwood Press
Westport, Connecticut . London, England

Library of Congress Cataloging in Publication Data

Winters, Donald E.
  The soul of the wobblies.

  Contributions in American studies, ISSN 0084-9227 ;
no. 81)
  Bibliography: p.
  Includes index.
  1. Industrial Workers of the World—History.
2. Church and labor—United States—History.
3. Sociology, Christian—United States—History.
4. United States—Social conditions—1865–1918.
I. Title. II. Series.
HD8055.I5W56   1985   331.88′6   84-27973
ISBN 0-313-24472-3 (lib. bdg.)

Library of Congress Catalog Card Number: 84-27973
ISBN: 0-313-24472-3
ISSN: 0084-9227

First published in 1985

Greenwood Press
A division of Congressional Information Service, Inc.
88 Post Road West, Westport, Connecticut 06881

Printed in the United States of America

10 9 8 7 6 5 4 3 2 1

Copyright Acknowledgments
Grateful acknowledgment is given for permission to use the following:

Stanzas from "Christians at War," "Out in the Breadline," "Hold the Fort,"
"The Lumberjack's Prayer," "The Preacher and the Slave," "There is Power
in the Union," "Casey Jones," "The Proletariare," and "All Hell Can't Stop
Us Now," along with excerpts from "Rebel's Toast," "Wesley Everest," "Joe
Hill: Murdered by the Authorities," "John Golden and the Lawrence Strike,"
"The God of Gold," and the I.W.W.'s Preamble are all printed here by per-
mission of the Industrial Workers of the World, 3435 N. Sheffield, Chicago,
Illinois 60657, USA.

I dedicate this book to the Industrial Workers of the World whose heroic legacy of struggle, sacrifice and militancy has earned them a permanent place in labor history and in American history.

Contents

Acknowledgments

Although numerous persons deserve thanks and gratitude, I will mention a few who come most immediately to mind. Most notably, I am deeply indebted to my wife, Julia Morgan, without whose love and support this study would have been impossible. Also, I am very grateful to two persons whose radical spirits and kind hearts helped me greatly during the writing of this work: Professor Mulford Q. Sibley, of the University of Minnesota, who gave me continuous encouragement during my research; and Fred Thompson, I.W.W. member and historian, who offered me his warm hospitality and assistance during the time that I spent at his home in Chicago.

I would also like to thank the good people at the special collections who helped me in my research, including Dione Miles, archivist at the Walter F. Reuther Library in Detroit; Edward C. Weber, head of the Labadie Collection at the University of Michigan; and Frank A. Zabrosky, curator at the University of Pittsburgh's Archives of Industrial Society. Also a special thanks goes to Diana Erickson whose skillful calligraphy appears in the appendix.

The Soul
of the
Wobblies

1

Introduction

In his introduction to *The Preacher and the Slave*, a 1950 novel about the I.W.W. martyr, Joe Hill, Wallace Stegner writes that "no thoroughly adequate history of the I.W.W. exists." Part of the reason for this, asserts Stegner, is that while the standard histories present valuable summaries of the Industrial Workers of the World's organization and activities, they are "lacking in the kind of poetic understanding which should invest any history of a militant church."[1] While this study does not purport to discuss the I.W.W., sometimes called the "Wobblies," as a "militant church" (such an attempt would invariably result in reductionism), it does seek to examine the relationship between the I.W.W. and American religion; or more specifically, between the I.W.W. and American Protestantism in the period from the union's formation in 1905 to America's entry into World War I in 1917.

There are several reasons for the choice of 1917 as the cutoff point for the period covered by this study. First, and the most significant, is the fact, pointed out clearly by Philip S. Foner, that although the I.W.W. still existed after World War I (and indeed still exists today), the repressive "alliance of big business and government . . . taking advantage of wartime hysteria" succeeded in destroying the effectiveness of the Union.[2] While Patrick Renshaw, in his book, *The Wobblies*, traces the I.W.W. until 1924, he admits that by then "the heart had gone out of the I.W.W."[3] and that the imprisonment of over a hundred Wobbly leaders between 1917–1918 was a blow from which the union would never recover and after which "the I.W.W. was never the same again."[4]

Secondly, the year 1917, besides marking the end of the effectiveness of the I.W.W. as a revolutionary union, marked the end of a unique interpenetration of secular and religious progressivism. As Cushing Strout points out in *The New Heavens and New Earth: Political Religion in America*:

The problem of distinguishing and relating secular and religious ideas in American reform movements of the late nineteenth and early twentieth centuries is a profoundly puzzling one . . . some advocates of Christian socialism appear to be more socialist than Christian, while others appear to be more Christian than socialist.

Between them lies the group of reformers whose blending of secular and religious traditions defies all neat categories of distinction.[5]

Between 1890 and America's entry into World War I, the so-called Progressive Era and the Social Gospel movement intersected at many points. It is this intersection, in part, that provides the social setting and points to the central tension crucial to this study. Although the Social Gospel or Social Christianity emerged fully after the Civil War, partially in an attempt to give moral direction to the powerful force of industrial capitalism, it was the last decade of the nineteenth century, according to Charles Howard Hopkins, in his seminal 1940 work, *The Social Gospel in American Protestantism, 1865–1915*, in which the movement reached its peak. In this period, Hopkins writes, liberal religion gave "wholehearted acceptance" to Darwin's evolutionary theory, resulting in the "three clearly related ideas" of "the immanence of God, the organic or solidaristic view of society, and the presence of the Kingdom of Heaven on earth."[6]

These three ideas had social and philosophical implications for both the religious and the secular advocates of progressivism during this period. Not only liberal clergy but social workers, politicians, educators and editors were preaching the Gospel of Progressivism from 1890 to 1917.[7] Unlike the earlier progressive "revolutions" of the Jeffersonian and Jacksonian eras, "the progressivism of the late nineteenth century had a religious sanction."[8]

Since this is neither a study of the Social Gospel movement nor of the Progressive Era *per se*, suffice it here to say that both movements grew out of an urgent desire to reassess and reform America's political and economic institutions. In the 1890's, Hopkins writes, "sociology and reform were quite compatible partners and the Social Gospel was a happy ally of both."[9] The Industrial Workers of the World, while engaging in rhetorical and political combat with all sides of the alliance, was, in some respects, more at home with religion—or at least its own radical, prophetic version of religion—than with the middle-class, political forces of "progressive" reform.

The third reason for selecting 1917 as this study's closing date is that the revolution in the Soviet Union in November of that year "provided a new focus for the world revolutionary cause."[10] Although most of the Wobblies were exhilarated by this historical event, only a few of them—most notably Bill Haywood and, later, Elizabeth Gurley Flynn—actually joined the Communist movement. The majority of members, however, rejected the Bolshevik Revolution as a model for the I.W.W. to follow because of its emphasis on political action and state power. This rejection, writes James P. Cannon, an I.W.W. organizer who was converted to Bolshevism, "sealed the doom of the I.W.W." as "the newly formed Communist Party soon outstripped the I.W.W. and left it on the sidelines."[11] Although Cannon's remarks must be seen in the context of his partisanship for revolutionary Marxism, his attitude is shared by non-Marxist critics of the I.W.W. from Gambs to Renshaw.[12]

LITERATURE

In his 1960 dissertation on the theories, organizational problems and appeals of the I.W.W., Thomas McEnroe writes of the "bare handful of monographs on the organization."[13] Indeed, with the exception of the five books he mentions,[14] McEnroe was writing his dissertation before the publication of most of the major works on the I.W.W. A growing interest during the 1960's in a radical critique of the American labor movement and in American history generally, produced such detailed histories as *The Industrial Workers of the World, 1905– 1917* by Philip Foner (1965), *The Wobblies: The Story of Syndicalism in the United States* by Patrick Renshaw (1967), *Rebels of the Woods* by Robert L. Tyler (1967) and *We Shall Be All* by Melvyn Dubofsky (1969). Also Joyce Kornbluh published in 1964 *Rebel Voices*, the first and only anthology of I.W.W. writing; and Joseph Conlin published in 1969 *Bread and Roses, Too*, intended as "a supplement to, rather than a successor of, the works of Brissenden, Foner, Renshaw, Tyler and others."[15]

These final two works are valuable in providing not general histories but frameworks for further critical, cultural scholarship on the I.W.W. While Conlin seeks to clarify some of the problems and myths facing historians, Kornbluh, by offering a rich collection of articles, cartoons, poems, songs and other works by the Wobblies themselves, contributes a valuable "starting point for additional research into the literature and lore of the I.W.W. that will explore its impact on American Society."[16]

It is the purpose of this study not only to examine the I.W.W.'s impact on American society and culture, but also to assess the reciprocal impact of American culture—particularly American religion at the beginning of the twentieth century—upon the I.W.W. Although it will be necessary to draw upon the secondary sources mentioned earlier, especially those written in the 1960's, the main source will be the "literature and lore" of the Wobblies themselves. Through an analysis of I.W.W. newspapers, autobiographies, songs and poems, I will attempt to assess the I.W.W. in relation to radical (and not so radical) American religious thought in the Progressive Era.

As Joseph Conlin points out in his two-volume collection of essays on America's radical press, "the Wobblies had a compulsion to publish newspapers" and are estimated to have produced sixty-six publications between 1905 and 1919.[17] The *Industrial Worker*, because of the length of time and the period in which it was published, will play a particularly significant role in this study. Published in Spokane and Seattle between 1909 and 1918,[18] the *Industrial Worker* (hereafter abbreviated *IW*) helped preach the message of industrial unionism to lumberjacks, farmworkers and copper miners of the West and Midwest. The earlier *Industrial Union Bulletin* (abbreviated *IUB*), published in Chicago from 1907 to 1909, was edited by the members of the general executive board. Together, the *IW* and *IUB* cover eleven years of the thirteen-year period of this study and represent the views of both the Eastern and Western Wobblies.[19] Since this study will be more concerned with broad cultural and religious issues than with geographic differences, less attention will be paid to whether an article, cartoon or poem appears in one paper or another than to what it has to say about the I.W.W. and American Progressive Era culture beyond the confines of geography. These two newspapers, together with the private and public writings of Wobblies, inside and outside the official press, will provide this study's primary source material.

PROBLEMS AND METHODOLOGY

One of the main problems that emerges when one attempts to discuss the relationship between religion and a revolutionary labor movement is the temptation to engage in the "reductionist fallacy" of equating one with the other. Wallace Stegner leaps headlong into this fallacy when he refers to the I.W.W. as a militant church. He does not say, unfortunately, that the I.W.W. possesses certain qualities of a church or that it is, in some ways, church-like, but that it is a militant church. Such an equation misrepresents the revolutionary, largely agnostic quality of the I.W.W. while broadening the use of the term "church" to such an extent that it lacks any substantial meaning. Fred Thompson, currently the primary internal historian of the I.W.W., made the following satirical remarks about the Wobblies-church equation:

There are points on which one can compare the I.W.W. and a church. In both, people congregate for fellowship and for the assertion and preservation of values, but I think it ends there unless you go to such points as that walls are vertical, supporting roofs in both cases, seating arrangements much the same, and even meeting procedures an-thropologically comparable. Our whole culture, including even our cussing, has been church-shaped.[20]

Although Thompson is certainly justified in disputing any attempts to draw an "I.W.W. = church" equation, there are parallels that go beyond the realms of fellowship and propagation of values and certainly beyond the *reductio absurdum* of seating arrangements and structure of walls. If one examines the autobiographical writings of Wobblies themselves, one finds striking and diverse comments on the relationship between religion and the Industrial Workers of the World.

In her autobiography, *Rebel Girl*, Elizabeth Gurley Flynn, perhaps the youngest I.W.W. organizer, writes that "the memorable accusation against Jesus, 'He stirrith up the people,' fitted the I.W.W."[21] Elsewhere, in speaking of her confinement in the Women's House of Detention for her labor activities, Flynn admits that the matron at the institution was, to a certain extent, correct when she said to her, after inquiring about her religion, "I guess socialism has always been your religion."[22]

William D. "Big Bill" Haywood, one of the union's most colorful and widely publicized leaders, followed a course similar to Flynn's, choosing to reject organized religion in favor of industrial unionism. In his autobiography, Haywood tells about how his boyhood confirmation in the Episcopal church of his mother was "the last time I attended a church service."[23] Near the end of this book, when writing about his arrest with several other I.W.W. members in 1917 following the U.S. declaration of war, he records how "some of the boys, when asked about their religion, answered 'the Industrial Workers of the World.'" When the guards challenged their response, according to Haywood, they replied: "Well, that's the only religion I've got."[24]

Ralph Chaplin, author of "Solidarity Forever" and numerous other Wobbly tunes, was one of the I.W.W. leaders arrested with Bill Haywood in 1917. Chaplin, a self-professed atheist[25] who nevertheless writes of his discovery of Whitman's *Leaves of Grass* as a "religious experience,"[26] says in his autobiography that the Industrial Workers of the World, "un-like orthodox Marxists . . . had no revolutionary Bible. Our simple creed was summed up in the *Little Red Song Book*, the I.W.W. Preamble, and a handful of ten-cent pamphlets." "The Preamble," he continues, "came first in our affections. It was at once our Declaration of Freedom and the tablets of the Law."[27]

In a similar vein, James Cannon, the I.W.W. organizer who became a leader of the American Trotskyist movement, wrote that the I.W.W. often became for the workers "their one all sufficient organization—their union and their party; their social center; their home; their family; their school; and in a manner of speaking, their religion, without the supernatural trimmings—the faith they lived by."[28] Cannon's phrases "a religion without the supernatural trimmings" and "the faith they lived by" indicate the thrust of this study. But first, it is essential to address the second problem suggested by Fred Thompson's remark and the autobiographical comments from other Wobblies: how does one define religion?

In order to avoid the reductionism Thompson writes about, it is necessary to have at least a fairly concrete working definition from which to proceed. Most of the sociological definitions are not suitable to this study because of their concern primarily with church-oriented analysis. Ronald L. Johnstone's *Religion and Society in Interaction*, for example, offers a working definition of religion as a "system of beliefs and practices by which a group of people interprets and responds to what they feel is supernatural and sacred." Johnstone has chosen this definition, he states, because it is "pragmatic" and "in tune with what the majority of people consider religion to be."[29]

Such definitions stem from the sociological assumption—held also by Robert Lee and Martin Marty in *Religion and Social Conflict* (1964) and Charles Glock and Rodney Stark in *Religion and Society in Tension* (1965)—that religion is usually impossible to discuss when removed from the institution of a church. In his book *The Invisible Religion*, sociologist Thomas Luckmann admits that in the "new sociology of religion . . . the definition of research problems and programs is, typically, determined by the institutional forms of traditional church organization."[30]

Part of Luckmann's criticism of the "new sociology of religion" is central to the methodology of this study. While political and economic phenomena are defined, says Luckmann, "by functional rather than substantial criteria . . . this is not generally the case for religion."[31] Recent sociologists of religion, states Luckmann, produce misleading general and substantive definitions of it because of their insistence on "a particular historical form of religion."[32] Such a narrow definition of religion would be of little value to this study since, as Henry F. May and many others have pointed out, the I.W.W. has expressed "a bitter suspicion of religion, a hatred of 'pie in the sky.' "[33]

If one is to discuss the Industrial Workers of the World in relation to American religion, one must necessarily take into consideration this suspicion, which was held by most Wobblies and which found its way into many of their songs, articles, autobiographies and speeches. It is also essential, in discovering instances where the I.W.W. was influenced by religious values or imagery, that one form a working definition that is both functional and radical, one that is compatible with the sense of religion that Wobblies like Elizabeth Gurley Flynn and Bill Haywood intend in their autobiographies.

Paul Tillich, Protestant theologian and Christian socialist, comes closer than most to the mark with his comments on "the anthropology of religious socialism" that seeks a philosophical basis lying "between the materialistic and idealistic conceptions of man" and suggests the following dual starting point: "The unity of that which is vital and spiritual in man, and the simultaneous disruption of the unity" which threatens man's very being.[34]

This disruption is central to the Wobblies' notion of class struggle. For the I.W.W., as stressed in their Preamble, "the working class and the employing class have nothing in common" and must engage in a continuous struggle "until the workers of the world organize as a class . . . [and] take possession of the earth and the machinery of production." In contrast to the "disruption" of the class struggle, the I.W.W. holds firmly to the virtue of solidarity which, to use Tillich's words, represents "the unity of that which is vital and spiritual in man." Solidarity is the "ultimate concern" of the Wobblies; and that is, in Tillich's terms, the value which is taken "with ultimate seriousness, unconditional seriousness."[35]

If the Industrial Workers of the World is to be viewed, in any sense, as religious, the central tenet of its faith must be seen as solidarity—a solidarity that lies somewhere between Bellamy's "religion of solidarity," with its passion for losing oneself in others,[36] and Georges Sorel's syndicalist ideology of solidarity, with its radicalizing myth of the general strike and its inherent acceptance of violence.[37]

The working definition of religion, then, that will serve for this study is as follows: a system of beliefs and symbols which seeks to develop in the working class a sense of solidarity and class consciousness, and a motivation to engage in a class struggle against the evil force of capitalism toward the end of creating a new order, a "commonwealth of toil," in the shell of the old. This definition, while certainly too limiting to suggest all the implications of this study, provides a functional starting point from which to begin. Also, the definition is solid enough, perhaps, to begin to draw the lines of demarcation between the I.W.W. and both the Social Gospel movement and progressivism while demonstrating its relationships to both.

In the following chapter, which examines the dialectical and religious nature of Wobbly solidarity, two prominent figures in the formation of the union—Eugene Debs and Father Hagerty—are discussed as early pioneers of the unique brand of prophetic radicalism that the I.W.W. would adopt. Chapters 3, 4 and 5 analyze more specifically the religious motif as it appears in I.W.W. songs, newspapers and poetry. Chapter 6 moves from the broad to the local by examining the implications of a particular Wobbly-led strike—the 1916 strike on Minnesota's Mesabi Range—for a particular community, the immigrant Finnish population, and its religious values. Finally, Chapter 7 concludes by assessing the place of the I.W.W. in American labor history and discussing the relationship between the Wobblies, progressives, and utopian novelists in the period preceding World War I.

NOTES

1. Wallace Stegner, *The Preacher and the Slave* (Boston: Houghton Mifflin Co., 1950), p. vii.

2. Philip S. Foner, *The Industrial Workers of the World, 1905–1917* (New York: International Publishers, 1965), pp. 558 and 10.

3. Patrick Renshaw, *The Wobblies: The Story of Syndicalism in the United States* (New York: Doubleday and Co., 1967), p. 238.

4. Ibid., p. 3.

5. Cushing Strout, *The New Heavens and New Earth: Political Religion in America* (New York: Harper and Row, 1974), pp. 225–226.

6. Charles Howard Hopkins, *The Social Gospel in American Protestantism, 1865–1915* (New Haven: Yale University Press, 1940), p. 123.

7. This relationship has already been discussed in several works, such as Henry F. May's *Protestant Churches and Industrial America* (particularly the chapter entitled "Social Gospel and American Progressivism"), Hopkins' book (see chapter "Sociology in the Service of Religion") and David Noble's *The Progressive Mind*.

8. Henry F. May, *Protestant Churches and Industrial America* (New York: Octagon Books, 1963), p. 225.

9. Hopkins, p. 257.

10. Renshaw, p. 197.

11. James P. Cannon, *The I.W.W.* (New York: Merit Publishers), p. 11.

12. Renshaw, p. 197, John S. Gambs' *The Decline of the I.W.W.*, "Communism and Internationalism," pp. 75–98 and Melvyn Dubofsky, *We Shall Be All*, p. 44.

13. Thomas H. McEnroe, *The Industrial Workers of the World: Theories, Organizational Problems, and Appeals as Revealed Principally in the "Industrial Worker"* (Minneapolis: University of Minnesota, August 1960), p. 6.

14. Paul F. Brissenden's *The I.W.W.: A Study of American Syndicalism*, John S. Gambs' *The Decline of the I.W.W.*, Fred Thompson's *The I.W.W.: Its First Fifty Years (1905–1955)*, John Graham Brooks' *American Syndicalism: The I.W.W.*, and Andre Tridon's *The New Unionism*.

15. Joseph Conlin, *Bread and Roses, Too* (Westport, Connecticut: Greenwood Publishing Co., 1969), p. xiv.

16. Joyce Kornbluh, *Rebel Voices* (Ann Arbor: University of Michigan Press, 1964), p. vi.

17. Joseph Conlin, *American Radical Press*, V.1 (Westport, Connecticut: Greenwood Press, 1974), p. 131.

18. Ibid., pp. 103–108. It is today published in Chicago as the official organ of the I.W.W.

19. Ibid., pp. 99–102. Brissenden, like many of the more recent I.W.W. scholars, discusses the West-vs.-East issue in the union and Robert Tyler presents an excellent study of the Western I.W.W. in *Rebels of the Woods*.

20. Letter sent to me dated February 24, 1978.

21. Elizabeth Gurley Flynn, *Rebel Girl* (New York: International Publishers, 1955), p. 77.

22. Ibid., p. 44.

23. William D. Haywood, *The Autobiography of Big Bill Haywood* (New York: International Publishers, 1929), p. 18.

24. Ibid., p. 304.

25. Ralph Chaplin, *Wobbly: The Rough-and-Tumble Story of an American Radical* (Chicago: University of Chicago Press, 1948), p. 275.

26. Ibid., p. 98.

27. Ibid., p. 147.

28. Cannon, *The I.W.W.*, p. 21.

29. Ronald L. Johnstone, *Religion and Society in Interaction* (Englewood Cliffs, New Jersey: Prentice Hall, 1975), p. 20.

30. Thomas Luckmann, *The Invisible Religion* (New York: Macmillan Co., 1967), p. 18.

31. Ibid., p. 42.

32. Ibid., p. 41.

33. May, *Protestant Churches*, p. 261.

34. Paul Tillich, *Political Expectation* (New York: Harper and Row, 1971), p. 46.

35. D. Mackenzie Brown, *Ultimate Concern: Tillich in Dialogue* (New York: Harper and Row, 1965), p. 7.

36. Edward Bellamy, *Selected Writings on Religion and Society* (New York: Liberal Arts Press, 1955), pp. 22–23.

37. Both Bellamy's essay "Religion of Solidarity," and (briefly) Sorel's *Reflections on Violence* will be discussed in the next chapter.

2

Father Hagerty, Comrade Debs, and the Dialectic of Solidarity

The founding convention of the Industrial Workers of the World, held in late June and early July of 1905, was an important, if frequently unsung, event in American labor and radical history. Although attended by some two hundred socialist and revolutionary delegates of various persuasions, that first convention "rang with the dominant notes of a handful of men."[1] Two of the early pioneers, Thomas J. Hagerty and Eugene V. Debs, were to play a dramatic role in the launching of the I.W.W., even though their direct involvement with the revolutionary union was brief. Both of these men, besides being passionately committed to socialism and industrial unionism, arrived at their ideological positions, at least in part, through the teachings of Christianity. Examining briefly the political histories of Hagerty and Debs will illustrate how an organization like the I.W.W., often violently opposed to all forms of organized religion, frequently derived its critique of capitalist America through a radical, prophetic interpretation of Christianity. Furthermore, an examination of the concepts of *solidarity* and *individualism*, two terms often subject to vigorous discussion and redefinition during the Progressive Era, will begin to illustrate the relationship between the I.W.W. and American religion in the opening decades of the twentieth century.

Solidarity was a virtue which the I.W.W. elevated above all others. Thomas J. Hagerty, perhaps the most influential single voice in the early shaping of the union, shared the faith of Eugene Debs that "without solidarity nothing is possible . . . with it nothing is impossible."[2] In his address before the opening convention, Hagerty spoke emphatically of class solidarity, declaring that,

in spite of petty national lines, in spite of international division lines, the workers of the world over are coming together on the ground of their common working class interest, without regard to race, color, creed or flag, and they are coming together because the earth and all the earth holds and all its possibilities are theirs. . . .[3]

Unlike Debs, however, Hagerty was a virtual newcomer to the socialist movement. In fact, until a little more than a year before the I.W.W.'s founding, he was Father Thomas Hagerty, a Roman Catholic priest.

Around 1892, three years before his ordination, Thomas Hagerty discovered, upon reading Marx's *Das Kapital* "with illuminating swiftness," the "complete answer to the questions [he] hardly partially solved" through more moderate texts.[4] He did not, however, immediately take up the banner of activism for the working class. In fact, in 1902, Father Hagerty could be found "going about his duties as assistant to the rector of Our Lady of Sorrows Catholic Church in Las Vegas, New Mexico [where he had been assigned the previous year] saying mass, hearing confessions, and baptising infants."[5]

In May of that year, however, Father Hagerty left his parish in Las Vegas, without permission from his superiors, to attend the joint meeting of the Western Labor Union and the Western Federation of Miners in Denver, Colorado. After spending the summer visiting mining camps, campaigning for the Socialist Party with Debs and generally urging the workers to revolt against their capitalist oppressors, Father Hagerty learned that he had been suspended from his religious duties by the Archbishop of Santa Fe.[6] However, in a letter to A. M. Simons, another founding father of the I.W.W. and then editor of the *International Socialist Review*, Hagerty insisted that despite his suspension, "I am as much a priest today as I ever was. I have not separated myself from the communion of the Catholic Church, and I hold myself as much a member thereof as the Pope himself."[7]

Such a statement had for Father Hagerty more political than religious significance. Since he planned to continue his traveling and agitation on behalf of the Socialist Party, Hagerty wished to serve as a living example to the working class that, despite Pope Leo's widely preached 1891 encyclical, *Rerum Novarum*, with its stinging denunciation of socialism,[8] there are some representatives of Christ who view socialism as a means of salvation and solidarity. It is unfortunate, Father Hagerty wrote in his letter to Simons, that a handful of bishops and priests "have seen fit to attack the principles of socialism, but it does not follow that the doctrines of the church, as such, are in conflict with the truths of socialism."[9]

For Hagerty, the two were not in conflict because they were concerned with different things. As he colorfully phrased it in his letter to Simons

No one would dream of going into a meat market asking for a Catholic beefsteak, a Methodist mutton chop, or a Presbyterian ham. Religion has no more to do with Socialism than it has with meat and bread. Socialism is an economic science, not a system of dogmatic beliefs. It is wholly beyond the scope of the Church's mission to deal with questions of social economy, just as it is beyond the purpose of the Republican party to advance a new exegesis of the Davidic Psalm.[10]

Or, as he put it a year later, in expressing his strong antipathy toward the Christian Socialists:

They would have men led into the highways of industrial righteousness by the allurement of Gospel texts, unmindful of the fact that nineteen centuries of such bandishment have failed to soften the granite heart of the ruling classes. The New Testament was never designed to serve as a treatise on socialism any more than it was intended to teach the first principles on biology.[11]

By the middle of 1904, no longer able to reconcile his role in the church with his increasingly radical, syndicalist political beliefs, Father Hagerty severed all connection with the Roman Catholic Church.[12] As he was to write in the American

Labor Union's *Voice of Labor*, "a new machine affects the world's ethics more profoundly than dozens of volumes of theology . . . the law of economic determination is stronger than dogma and greater than artificial moralities."[13] Although such an affirmation of materialism might seem antithetical to any form of Christian morality, Hagerty does not, despite his break from the church, abandon Christianity entirely. Instead, his faith seems to take on an increasingly prophetic cast.

The prophetic approach, as I will discuss in greater detail later, lends itself more easily to an ethic of solidarity than does church-oriented religion. The prophetic writers of the Old Testament were more concerned with society as a whole than with the individual believer.[14] Furthermore, Hagerty found the spirit of prophecy an effective rhetorical weapon in addressing the working class, a class historically suspicious of organized religion, about the "false prophets" who try to deceive them.[15] In the January 1, 1905, issue of *Voice of Labor*, for example, Hagerty denounces soundly the Colorado Baptists who, at their state convention, reprimanded strikers for inhibiting "the progress of God's work." In an article entitled "A Howl from the Pharisees," Hagerty angrily assures the "Pharisee" preachers that,

in spite of their cringing obsequiousness to the Citizen's Alliance and the Mine Owners' Association in denouncing the strike of the Western Federation of Miners, the churchmen of Colo-Russia have not been able to stampede the ranks of the strikers.

The preachers had also failed, Hagerty writes, "to soothe the discontent of the working class by assurances of a happy and plentiful hereafter in exchange for contentment, rags and hunger in the lean and sullen present."[16]

At the founding convention of the I.W.W., six months later, Thomas Hagerty presented a striking figure that was both commanding and prophetic. No single person was more influential in shaping the form which the union took. As secretary of the convention's constitution committee, he played a major role in framing the Industrial Union Manifesto, which urged all members to revolt against craft unionism and capitalism.[17]

Furthermore, Thomas Hagerty, along with James T. Thompson and a few others, composed the controversial Preamble.[18] This famous document of American revolutionary literature, which begins by asserting that the working class and the employing class have nothing in common, was probably the most widely read I.W.W. statement. Appearing in almost every issue of the *Little Red Songbook* as well as the union's press, it created anger and fear among employers and controversy within the ranks of the I.W.W., particularly concerning the political clause added by Daniel De Leon.[19] The spirit of this historical document resembles, in tone, the prophetic books of the Old Testament with its emphasis on existing social ills and its warning about corrupt leaders of the people.[20]

Like Hagerty, Eugene V. Debs was "one of the leading spirits in the organization of the I.W.W. in 1905."[21] An ardent admirer of this "brave and intellectual priest," Debs counted Hagerty "in the giant group that is destined to blaze the way to the new emancipation and glorify the age with their immortal achievements."[22] Rather than relate in detail the radical history of Debs, which is much more widely known and accessible than Hagerty's, I will focus on the unique religiosity of this great leader of the socialist movement, particularly as it deviates from Hagerty's and sheds light on the individualism/solidarity dialectic that characterized the I.W.W.

Debs was born in Terre Haute, Indiana in 1855. Dropping out of high school at fourteen, he entered the working class at an early age, working in a railroad paint shop from 1871 to 1874. In 1875 he joined the Brotherhood of Locomotive Firemen and served as the first secretary of the Terre Haute local.[23] In 1894 the American Railway Union was organized and, as Debs put it in *Comrade* magazine, "a braver body of men never fought the battle of the working class."[24] It was in the A.R.U. that Debs played an important leadership role in the Pullman strike which resulted in his six-month jail sentence in the Woodstock, Illinois, jail for violating an anti-strike court injunction. "I was to be baptised in socialism in the roar of conflict," Debs wrote in *Comrade*, "and I thank the gods for reserving to this fitful occasion the fiat, 'Let there be light!'—

the light that streams in steady radiance upon the broad way to the socialist republic."[25]

Like his socialism, Debs' religion developed out of his immediate experience. As biographer Ray Ginger writes, Debs "was among a deeply religious folk [who] had learned about Marxism from the populizers of Karl Marx" and "about Christianity from the tent preachers of the Midwest."[26] Or, as Debs' authorized biographer Daniel Karsner writes: "Debs is a most religious man. He accepts literally what he conceives to be the principles for which Christ was crucified. He is a Christian to whom the Church offers nothing but an apology for Christ."[27]

The Christ Debs admired, in other words, was certainly not the Christ worshipped in the sermons and masses of organized religion, but was the "master proletarian revolutionist and sower of the social whirlwind"; he was the "grandest and loftiest of human souls—as real, as palpitant, and as pervasive an historic character as John Brown, Abraham Lincoln, and Karl Marx."[28] This is the Christ Debs spoke of with two clergy members when they came to visit him in his cell in Moundville Prison (Atlanta), where he was serving time in 1919 for making anti-war speeches. In discussing the incident with David Karsner, then a young reporter for the New York *Call*, he pointed to the picture of Christ he had next to his bed and told the young reporter,

I told my friends of the cloth that I did not believe Christ was meek and lowly but a real, living, vital agitator who went into the temple with a lash and a krout and whipped the oppressors of the poor, routed them out of doors and spilled their blood and got silver on the floor. He told the robbed and misruled and exploited and driven people to disobey their plunderers, he denounced the profiteers, and it was for this that they nailed his quivering body to the cross and spiked it to the gates of Jerusalem, not because he told them to love one another. That was a harmless doctrine. But when he touched their profits and denounced them before their people he was then marked for crucifixion.[29]

This passage illustrates a popular image of Jesus that pervades both the literature of the I.W.W. and social Christianity throughout the Progressive Era. It is an image that suggests the points of similarity and difference between the I.W.W. and the Social Gospel movement as well as cultural justification available to the Wobblies in defending their ideas about solidarity and individualism.

Both Father Hagerty and Eugene Debs, like the Social Gospel movement and the I.W.W., fit into the religious tradition of a humanized image of Jesus. When the first edition of *The Political and Social Significance of the Life and Teachings of Jesus* by Jeremiah W. Jenks came out in 1906, and Joseph A. Leighton's *Jesus Christ and the Civilization of Today* the following year, they were enthusiastically received by the public.[30] These interpretations went to the heart of Christian social teaching arguing, as Jenks asserts, that "His Kingdom must go deeper than mere political form; it must put a new soul into society" that eliminates all social class.[31]

Although both Hagerty and Debs, when alluding to Jesus or his teachings, depicted a rebel Jesus who "stirreth up the masses," the two early pioneers of the I.W.W. disagreed about whether or not Christianity and socialism were compatible. As mentioned, Hagerty became increasingly more convinced every day that while the two were not necessarily in conflict, they ought to be concerned with different things: socialism with economic matters and religion with the spiritual side of man. Debs, on the other hand, saw them as perfectly complementary; and, while Hagerty mocked the Christian Socialists for attempting to find a socialist message in the New Testament, Debs was able to address the 1908 conference of the Christian Socialist Fellowship with the following words: "A few years ago, a meeting like this would have been impossible. . . . I'm glad I can now call you ministers of the Man of Galilee my comrades, for it isn't long ago that I felt a great prejudice against you as a class."[32]

Such a peace-making statement illustrates why Henry F. May is able to say that in spite of the hostility between the churches and the radical labor movement, "an occasional labor leader like Eugene Debs has been able to work with both groups, combining in himself the bitter experience of the left-wing rank and file with strong ethical, semi-religious motivations."[33] It also explains, however, why a Wobbly writer like Ralph V.

Chervinski was to say of Debs in 1912: "Being a sentimental-ist himself he cannot understand the absence of sentiment in others. He condemns such absence as morbid and reaction-ary. . . . He looks upon the things of TODAY with the eyes of the PAST—and he BELONGS TO THE PAST." (*IW* 2/22/12, p. 4).

Despite the I.W.W.'s often-stated opposition to organized re-ligion, there are numerous points where the union's atti-tudes—expressed through its journalism, songs, cartoons and speeches—are in almost complete agreement with the more radical leaders of the Social Gospel movement. Walter Raus-chenbusch, for example, in his well-known 1912 book, *Chris-tianizing the Social Order*, frequently criticizes the capitalis-tic advocates of economic individualism while supporting a socialist variety of economic solidarity throughout his work. "To concentrate our efforts on personal salvation as orthodoxy has done," writes Rauschenbusch, "or on soul culture as liberal-ism has done, comes close to refined selfishness. . . . Our personality is of divine and external value, but we see it aright only when we see it as part of mankind. Our religious individ-uality must get its interpretation from the supreme fact of so-cial solidarity."[34] In his earlier work, *Christianity and the So-cial Crisis* (1907), he offers the following comments on the Old Testament prophets as a worthwhile lesson in solidarity for Americans to heed:

The Prophets were not religious individualists. During the classical times of prophetism they always dealt with Israel and Judah as or-ganic totalities. They conceived of their people as a gigantic person-ality which sinned as one and ought to repent as one. When they speak of their nation as a virgin, as a city, as a vine, they are attempting by these figures of speech to express this organic and corporate social life . . . the prophets were public men and their interest was in pub-lic affairs.[35]

The Social Gospel Christians, such as Washington Gladden, George Herron, Richard Ely and Walter Rauschenbusch, preached the gospel of solidarity as opposed to the gospel of individualism, Social Darwinism or *laissez-faire* capitalism. In the two-party system within Protestantism, noted originally by

Gladden in 1913, the Social Gospel movement would fit within the "party" of Social Christianity, while the evangelical Protestants like Dwight Moody fit into the "traditional, familiar, and dominant" party of individualist Christianity.[36] While conservatives usually insisted that Christian tradition was on their side while Social Christianity was suspiciously new, radicals like Rauschenbusch argued that the tradition of Social Christianity had much deeper roots in Christian soil than the evangelicals; roots that could be traced to the prophetic Hebrew scriptures and the Jesus of the Synoptic Gospels. "The sympathy of the prophets," wrote Rauschenbusch, "even the most aristocratic among them, was entirely on the side of the poorer classes."[37]

The prophetic tradition, in its great concern for social justice, rejected the "pie-in-the-sky" attitude frequently found among the conservatives and strongly opposed by the Wobblies in such famous songs as "The Preacher and the Slave." "The belief in a future life and future reward and punishment was almost absent in Hebrew religion," Rauschenbusch asserts, "God must prove his justice here or never . . . [but] in Christianity, faith in the future life has to some extent subdued the demand for social justice."[38]

It is the prophetic element of the Social Gospel movement that is in harmony with much of the spirit of the Wobblies. But when social Christians like Rauschenbusch, perhaps the most astute student of socialism in the movement, begin to make concrete proposals for the tactics and strategies of social change, a very wide chasm emerges between him and radical industrial unionists like Debs and Hagerty.[39]

On the matter of strikes, for example, both the Social Gospel movement and a large portion of the primarily middle-class Progressive movement looked upon them as dangerous activities, as manifestations of class antagonism and social extremes, which both movements sought to avoid.[40] "The economic loss to both sides in every strike is great enough," Rauschenbusch warns, "but the loss of human fellowship and kindliness is of far greater moment. The acts of violence committed on both sides . . . is all brutalizing and destructive. If our industrial organization cannot evolve some saner method of reconciling conflicting interests than twenty-four thousand strikes and lockouts in twenty years, it will be a confession of social impotence and moral bankruptcy."[41]

On a similar note, Theodore Roosevelt, the most influential representative of political Progressivism, said the following about strikes and labor disputes in his 1917 book, *The Foes of Our Own Household*:

In any labor disturbance of a size or character to jeopardize the public welfare, there are three parties in interest—the property owners, the wage earners and the general public. I refuse to assent to the view that either the owners of the property, or the workers, have interests paramount to the general interest of the public at large.[42]

While both Rauschenbusch and Roosevelt place the interest of the "general public" above the interest of the working class, the I.W.W. refuses to see society in this tripartite structure. The "general public," for the I.W.W., is part of the working class, and the "working class and the employing class have nothing in common." In an editorial entitled "Teddy the Tough," the *Industrial Worker* refers to a recent article in the *International Socialist Review* in which Social Gospel intellectual George Herron says of Theodore Roosevelt that "it is this one man, more than all others, who has awakened the instinct to kill and conquer . . . who has put the blood-cup to the lips of the nation and bids the nation to drink." Although the Wobbly writer agrees with Herron's assessment of Roosevelt, he argues that Herron, as a political socialist, is too concerned with the dangerous power of one political figure. "But it is not with [the political movement] that Roosevelt and his masters will have to reckon," says the *Worker*, "It is the red-blooded worker with NOTHING TO LOSE AND A CONTEMPT FOR CONSEQUENCES that will sweep away the rottenness and build a clean and wholesome structure that will have for its foundation the principle of 'to the worker the product of his toil.'" (*IW* 6/11/10, p. 2)

Two other areas where the Social Gospel movement usually finds itself in agreement with political progressivism and at odds with the I.W.W. are proletarian autonomy and revolutionary class consciousness. "It is to the interest of all sides," Rauschenbusch writes, "that the readjustment of the social classes should come as a steady evolutionary process rather than as a social catastrophe." If the latter takes place rather than the former, worries Rauschenbusch, widespread disorder would develop, followed by a "reactionary relapse to old conditions."[43] Similarly, Theodore Roosevelt, after calling for "wise, moderate, steady action" as a cure for America's national ills, urges the nation to "remember that the demagogue is as dangerous a public enemy as the corruptionist himself, and that the insincere radical is not a whit better than the insincere Tory, and that the enthusiastic fool will probably work even more mischief than the selfish reactionary." For Roosevelt, the revolutionary, no less than the selfish businessman, is "among the foes of our own household."[44]

On the issue of class-struggle socialism, both Rauschenbusch and Roosevelt come out on similar territory. While Rauschenbusch, particularly in *Christianity and the Social Crisis*, gives lip service to socialism, Roosevelt vehemently exclaims,

The immorality and absurdity of the doctrine of socialism . . . are quite as great as those of the advocates of unlimited individualism. As an academic matter, Herbert Spencer stands as far to one side of the line of sane action as Marx stands on the other. But practically there is more need of refutation of the creed of absolute socialism than the creed of absolute individualism; for it happens that at the present time a greater number of visionaries, both sinister and merely dreamy, believe in the former than in the latter.[45]

While Rauschenbusch, like many of the Social Gospel preachers, sees "socialism . . . as the ultimate and logical outcome of the labor movement," he does not feel the workers can win the struggle by their own strength. The working class, in order to emerge victorious, must ally itself with the middle class. "Each depends on the other," says Rauschenbusch, "the idealistic movement alone would be a soul without a body; the economic class movement alone would be a body without a soul. It needs the high elation and faith that comes through religion."[46] The working class, for both the social Christians and the political Progressives, did not have the moral strength to liberate itself but must seek necessary guidance from middle class leaders of the church and the Progressive movement.

The Industrial Workers of the World, however, did not see the middle class as either a paragon of virtue or as the potential leadership for the New World Order or the Industrial Commonwealth. Although the I.W.W. was never very precise in its definition of class,[47] it is clear throughout its writings that the often vaguely defined "working class," not the middle class, will "arise like lions after slumber." (*IW* 11/7/12, p. 4) As another Wobbly writer strongly phrases it, "We are tired of the unctuous, sleek, self-satisfied, smirking, bourgeois-minded 'savior' [of the working class] . . . Let us be INDIVIDUAL-ISTS but individualists who are intelligent enough to see that our individualism is best served by cooperation, UNIONISM, an alliance with those whose interests are in harmony with ours." (*IW* "Sympathy" 5/21/10, p. 2)

In I.W.W. writing, there is an often dialectical relationship between solidarity and individualism. In order to clarify some of the complexities inherent in this relationship, it will be necessary to return again to the characters of Hagerty and Debs, both of whom viewed solidarity as the *summum bonum* for the building of a revolutionary, class-conscious labor movement. Also, for both of these men, as indeed for most members of the I.W.W., "solidarity" played almost the same role as a concept like "grace" plays for Christianity, with almost the same multiplicity of possible meanings.

For Eugene V. Debs, the most popular and influential member of the Socialist Party, "solidarity" was a term rich in religious significance. As one who believed in a dynamic interaction between Christian and socialist values, Debs would no doubt be quite amenable to Rauschenbusch's remark, in a 1914 article in the *Christian Socialist*, that "Christianity and Socialism are the oldest and youngest of the idealistic forces at work in our civilization. The future lies, not with those who choose either of the two, but with those who can effect the completest amalgamation of the two."[48] Indeed, by 1908, the year Debs addressed the members of the Christian Socialist

Fellowship as "comrades," it was claimed that more than 300 preachers belonged to the Socialist Party.[49]

Early in 1914, when the I.W.W. was divided into two factions and a good portion of the left-wing of America was engaged in ideological and political combat, Debs delivered a "Plea for Solidarity" in the pages of the *International Socialist Review*. "Solidarity," wrote Debs,

is not a matter of sentiment but a fact, cold and impassive as the granite foundation of a skyscraper. If the basic elements, identity of interest, clarity of vision, honesty of intent, and oneness of purpose, or any of these is lacking, all sentimental pleas for solidarity, and all other efforts to achieve it will be alike barren of results.[50]

Although Debs' efforts at bringing realignment to the revolutionary movement called for an unsentimental, non-sectarian definition of the term, the Wobbly writer Ralph Chervinski's charge, two years earlier, that Debs as a "sentimentalist himself" was not far from the truth. Debs' personal concept of solidarity, like a large part of his socialism, came from his experiences in social struggles as well as the diverse range of writers he became familiar with while in prison. One of the writers he read in Woodstock jail, according to his "How I became a Socialist" article, was Edward Bellamy.[51]

Since the only significant work published by Bellamy by 1895, the year Debs spent in Woodstock, was his famous 1888 novel, *Looking Backward*, this is very likely the work Debs is referring to. Like most of the Social Gospel fiction and tracts published in the 1880's, *Looking Backward* asks the question of why the ethics of the New Testament cannot be applied to society in the nineteenth century. Julian West, the main character of the novel, falls asleep in 1887 and awakens to find himself in the year 2000 where cut-throat competition has been replaced by "the solidarity of the race and the brotherhood of man." As Joseph Schiffman writes, in an introduction to Bellamy's collected writings, "Bellamy's utopia is a fascinating transformation of the millennium foretold by Hebrew prophets in the book of Daniel, and celebrated in the Psalms and in Isaiah."[52] In "The Religion of Solidarity," an essay written by Bellamy in 1874 but not published until 1940, forty-two years after his death, Bellamy sets down the "germ" of his philosophy. "In the religion of solidarity," Bellamy writes, "is found the only rational philosophy of moral instincts. Unselfishness, self-sacrifice, are the essence of morality. On the theory of ultimate individualities, unselfishness is madness."[53]

It is this spiritual form of solidarity, rather than the "cold and impassive" variety defined in his 1914 speech, that is most characteristic of Eugene Debs. It is, indeed, the kind of spirit that earned him the respect of the Christian Socialists, the labor radicals, and the nearly 6 percent of the voting public who cast almost a million votes for him in the 1920 presidential election. It is the self-sacrificing solidarity that permeates much of Debs' public speaking, perhaps most explicitly in the speech delivered in Girard, Kansas in 1908, the same year in which Debs addressed the Christian Socialist Fellowship and in which the Federal Council of Churches was founded, institutionalizing the Social Gospel movement. Debs begins his speech by posing the scriptural question: "Am I my brother's keeper?" That frequently asked question, Debs says, "has never yet been answered in a way that is satisfactory to civilized society. Yes, I am my brother's keeper. I am under a moral obligation to him that is inspired, not by maudlin sentimentality, but by the higher duty I owe to myself."[54] It is when one is helping one's brother that a person feels most alive, Debs insists, not when one is merely functioning as a wage slave. Debs continues:

It is when you have done your work honestly, when you have contributed your share to the common fund that you begin to live. Then, as Whitman said, you can take out your soul; you can commune with yourself; you can take a comrade by the hand and you can look into his soul, and in that holy communion you live. And if you don't know what that is, or if you are not at least on the edge of it, it is denied you to even look into the Promised Land.[55]

If Debs' brand of solidarity seems to project Bellamy's "religion of solidarity" and Christ's Sermon on the Mount (the "manifesto" of compassion for Social Christianity), the solidarity of Father Hagerty and the other syndicalists in the I.W.W. burns with the flame of prophecy and the rage of Christ's violent removal of the money-changers from the temple. A concrete example of this can be seen in the incident Debs relates about how Hagerty, while serving as a priest in Cleburne, Texas, stood up for the workers. When the "hirelings" of the railroad corporation tried to get the "brave and intellectual priest" to leave town, Hagerty responded with the warning: "Tell the people who sent you here that I have a brace of colts and can hit a dime at twenty paces."[56] This remark, though certainly not a precise political statement, nevertheless hints at the direct-action spirit of Hagerty who was influenced, like William E. Trautmann, another "leading spirit" of the early I.W.W., by the anarcho-syndicalist movement abroad.[57]

The conception of solidarity by direct-actionists like Hagerty has a far different spiritual character than the milder, more benevolent "religion of solidarity" held by the Social Christians and, to a certain extent, by Debs. The French syndicalists, which the *Industrial Worker* wrote of extensively in 1910, urging its readers to re-read the articles a dozen times (*IW* 9/27/10, p. 2), often stressed the spiritual value of direct-action for instilling solidarity among the working class. As European syndicalist Odor Por expressed it, the "limitless importance of syndicalism" is that it "creates, develops, focuses, and sets to work the productive and moral energies of man." (*IW* 5/1/12, p. 4) Of the French syndicalists, perhaps the most influential was Georges Sorel, whose most popular book, *Reflections on Violence*, was first published in 1908. It is mainly because of Sorel's writings that the concept of the "militant minority" underwent widespread debate among radicals in Europe and America.

Without discussing in great detail Sorel or the French syndicalists, reference to a few key passages of *Reflections* that deal with the question of solidarity and individualism is necessary. Since Foner and Brissenden have discussed syndicalism in depth, only a concise definition by William Z. Foster is included here.

In its basic aspects, syndicalism, or more properly anarcho-syndicalism, may be defined very briefly as that tendency in the labor movement to confine the revolutionary class struggle of the workers to the economic field, to practically ignore the state, and to reduce the whole fight of the working class to simply a question of trade union action. Its fighting organization is the trade union; its basic method of class warfare is the strike, with the general strike as the revolutionary weapon; and its revolutionary goal is the setting up of a trade union 'state' to conduct industry and all other social activities.[58]

In *Reflections*, Sorel attributes a powerful religious, mythical value to that "basic method of class warfare" which the Wobblies held in such high revolutionary regard: the general strike. The myth of the general strike, Sorel contends, can be legitimately compared to the myth of the second coming of Christ. "The first Christians," writes Sorel, "expected the return of Christ and the total ruin of the pagan world, with the inauguration of the kingdom of the saints at the end of the first generation. The catastrophe did not come to pass, but Christian thought profitted so greatly from the apocalyptic myth that certain contemporary scholars maintain that the whole preaching of Christ referred solely to this point." It is of little consequence, says Sorel, whether the general strike is historical reality or merely part of the proletariat imagination, since "it is the myth in its entirety which is alone important" and which provides "a means of acting on the present."[59] It also provides the prophetic framework, especially for the anarcho-syndicalists in the I.W.W., for a concept of working class solidarity.

For the political socialists, like Eugene Debs, the anarcho-syndicalist philosophy, which soon came to dominate the I.W.W., offered not a means for achieving solidarity but a road backward to an outdated individualism so soundly condemned by Bellamy, the Social Gospel movement, the socialists, and all other forces for change in the Progressive Era. Historian John Graham Brooks, writing in 1920, even went so far as to speculate whether the syndicalist "might be an agent provocateur of the capitalist" since he "certainly is his tool." The syndicalist tactics of "sabotage, destruction of industrial capital, perpetual strikes," writes Brooks, "injure the workers far more than any other class, and rouse in society reactionary passions and prejudices which defeat the work of every agency making for emancipation of labor."[60]

The I.W.W., Brooks believed, "was dangerous because it represented an anachronistic individualism, and because it refused to accept the organic nature of modern industrial and political life . . . [glorifying] impulse, 'direct action,' and class consciousness."[61] Similarly, Eugene Debs said in 1912:

I am opposed to sabotage and to 'direct action.' I have not a bit of use for the 'propaganda of the deed'. . . . The foolish and misguided zealots and fanatics are quick to applaud such tactics and the result is usually hurtful to themselves and to the cause they seek to advance.

Although Debs can conceive of moments in history where the "frenzied deed of a glorious fanatic like John Brown" who "seemed inspired by Jehovah himself" can be of positive value to the cause of justice, in the present century "such tactics appeal to stealth and suspicion, and cannot make for solidarity." (*IW* 2/22/12, p. 4)

In a series of thirteen articles on sabotage, printed in the *Industrial Worker* the following year, however, the I.W.W. denies that direct-action tactics such as sabotage destroy or even hinder solidarity. "The individual acts of sabotage," the article asserts, "performed to the end that class benefit be derived, can in no way militate against solidarity. Rather, they promote unity." (*IW* 3/27/13, p. 2) "The saboteur," another issue proclaims, "is the sharpshooter of the revolution" and sabotage itself is "the smokeless powder of the social war." (*IW* 3/6/13, p. 2) If the Wobblies are individualistic, it is an individualism reinforced with the sturdier stuff of which solidarity is made. "The general strike," says Sorel, "just like the war of Liberty, is a most striking manifestation of individualistic force in the revolted masses." It is the reclaiming of a "passionate individualism" which is "entirely lacking in the working classes who have been educated by politicians" until "all they are fit for is to change their masters."[62]

For most of the members of the I.W.W., individualism equalled "rebellion," a spiritual force essential in the worker's struggle against capitalism. In a union that received much of its strength from the rootless wanderers and migratory workers rather than a stable industrial work force, the image of the "hobo" and the "blanket stiff" were positive not negative. In an article entitled "The Floater, An Iconoclast," Wobbly leader Walker C. Smith writes:

When a large strike of long duration occurs in the east, the more rebellious of the unmarried men go west. The married men are tied by wife, children and property to their particular location and must stay, win or lose. Those young and unmarried men have within them the spirit of unionism rather than the desire for the craft form of organization. . . . These men are the casual, the migratory workers . . . their work shows them the direct relationship between cause and effect, and this destroys their belief in God. They are irreligious. Their words and ethics are not those of the ruling class. . . . A hatred for the priest, the soldier and other forms of authority is ever present. This is the class that masters fear. (*IW* 6/4/10, p. 2)

This statement illustrates a disturbing problem implicit in the Wobbly brand of individualism. In its rejection of the institutional barriers that confine workers to the chains of capitalism, the I.W.W. frequently viewed women and families in the same context as they did such "forms of authority" as the church, the military and craft unionism. This contradiction, which Philip Foner treats in *Women in the Labor Movement* (New York: Free Press, 1979), is recognized by Joe Hill when he warns the Western I.W.W. about becoming a "freak," removed from association with women.

One sees in dealing with I.W.W. songs, journalism and poetry, many of the traits of the rebellious "iconoclast", which Smith claims "destroys their faith in God" and makes them "irreligious," are the very traits which contribute to the creation of a kind of revolutionary religion in the I.W.W., combining the most radical features of "solidarity" and "individualism." For the I.W.W., these two qualities are dynamically interrelated, dialectically complementary. The militant figure of Jesus, who appears variously throughout Wobbly writing as an agitator, a hobo, a revolutionist,[63] combines both qualities in one man and often serves as the prophetic archetype of the rootless rebel. Unlike the Socialist Party, the Social Gospel or the Progressive Movements, the Industrial Workers of the World perceived an "irrepressible conflict between the capitalist class and the working class," as uncompromising as the battle between God and the Devil, which must continue until the workers of the world achieve emancipation.

NOTES

1. Paul F. Brissenden, *The I.W.W.: A Study of American Syndicalism* (New York: Russell and Russell, 1919), p. 79.

2. I.W.W., *The Founding Convention of the I.W.W.: Proceedings* (New York: Merit Publishers, 1905), p. 146.

3. Ibid., p. 570.

4. Thomas J. Hagerty, "How I Became a Socialist," *Comrade* (October 1902), pp. 6–7.

5. Robert E. Doherty, "Thomas J. Hagerty, the Church, and Socialism," *Labor History* (Winter 1962), pp. 39–40.

6. Ibid., pp. 42–43.

7. *International Socialist Review* (October 1902), p. 229.

8. John Graham Brooks, "The Papal Encyclical on the Labor Question," *Publications of the American Economic Association* (7th annual meeting, 1894), pp. 75–76. Also see Chapter 9 of Marc Karson's *American Labor Unions and Politics*, entitled "The Roman Catholic Church and American Labor Unions."

9. *International Socialist Review* (October 1902), p. 230.

10. Ibid., p. 229.

11. Hagerty, "Socialism vs. Fads," *International Socialist Review* (February 1903), p. 452.

12. Doherty, p. 53.

13. Hagerty, "Economic Determinism," *Voice of Labor* (February 1905), pp. 5–6.

14. J. Philip Hyatt, *Prophetic Religion* (New York: Abingdon-Cokesbury Press, 1947), p. 74.

15. After Marx, many Christians have made this observation. In 1907, for example, Walter Rauschenbusch says "it cannot be denied that there is an increasing alienation between the working class and the churches." (*Christianity and the Social Crisis*, p. 329). And more recently, in 1967, Thomas Luckmann, in *The Invisible Religion* (London: Macmillan, 1967), points out that, generally, "the degree of involvement in the work process of modern industrial society correlates negatively with the degree of involvement in church-oriented religion." (p. 30)

16. Hagerty, "A Howl from the Pharisees," *Voice of Labor* (January 1905), p. 16.

17. Doherty, p. 39.

18. Brissenden, p. 79 and Doherty, p. 55.

19. The debate between the pro-political minority (De Leonists) and anti-political majority rages throughout many of the 1907 issues of the *Industrial Union Bulletin*, finally resulting in a split in the 1908 Fourth Annual Convention. Patrick Renshaw, in *The Wobblies*, speaks of the deep-rooted aversion to any form of political action that has long characterized the American labor movement. (p. 9)

20. Thomas H. McEnroe's unpublished University of Minnesota dissertation, "The I.W.W.: Themes, Organizational Problems and Appeals, as Revealed Principally in *The Industrial Worker*" (1960), p. 129, compared the spirit of the Preamble with ideas appearing in Joachim of Fiore's *Eternal Gospel*.

21. Brissenden, p. 253.

22. Debs interview with Hagerty, "Hagerty on the Hustings," *American Labor Union Journal* (January 29, 1903), p. 6.

23. "Biographical Note" in Eugene V. Debs Speaks, edited by Jean Tussey (New York: Pathfinder Press, 1970), p. 46.

24. Eugene V. Debs, "How I Became a Socialist," *Comrade* (April 1902), reprinted in *Eugene V. Debs Speaks*, p. 46.

25. Ibid., pp. 46–47.

26. Ray Ginger, *The Bending Cross: A Biography of Eugene Victor Debs* (New York: Russell and Russell, 1949), p. 11.

27. Daniel Karsner, *Debs: His Authorized Life and Letters* (New York: Boni and Liveright, 1919), p. 11.

28. Ginger, p. 287.

29. Karsner, pp. 10–11.

30. Charles Howard Hopkins, *The Social Gospel in American Protestantism, 1865–1915* (New Haven: Yale University Press, 1940), pp. 206–207.

31. Jeremiah W. Jenks, *The Political and Social Significance of the Life and Teachings of Jesus* (New York: International Committee of Young Men's Christian Associations, 1906), p. 31.

32. Robert T. Handy, "Christianity and Socialism in America, 1900–1920," *Church History* (March 1952), p. 50.

33. Henry F. May, *Protestant Churches and Industrial America* (New York: Octagon Books, 1963), p. 261.

34. Walter Rauschenbusch, *Christianizing the Social Order* (New York: Macmillan, 1912), p. 465.

35. Walter Rauschenbusch, *Christianity and the Social Crisis*, ed. Robert D. Cross (New York: Harper Torchbook edition, 1964), pp. 8–9.

36. Discussed by Martin Marty in *Righteous Empire: The Protestant Experience in America* (New York: Dial Press, 1970), pp. 177–187.

37. Rauschenbusch, *Social Crisis*, p. 11.

38. Ibid., pp. 17–18.

39. In fact, on those occasions, one begins to realize why Sidney Ahlstrom refers to the Social Gospel movement as "the praying wing of Progressivism" (*Religious History of the American People*, p. 804).

40. Richard Hofstadter, *The Age of Reform: From Bryan to F.D.R.* (New York: Alfred Knopf, 1956), p. 242.

41. Rauschenbusch, *Social Crisis*, p. 239.

42. Theodore Roosevelt, *The Foes of Our Own Household* (New York: George H. Doran Co., 1917), pp. 116–117.

43. Rauschenbusch, *Social Crisis*, p. 410.

44. Roosevelt, *The Foes of Our Own Household*, pp. 144–145.

45. Ibid., p. 163.

46. Rauschenbusch, *Social Crisis*, pp. 408–409.

47. Melvyn Dubofsky, *We Shall Be All: A History of the I.W.W.* (New York: Quadrangle, 1969), p. 152.

48. Quoted by Robert T. Handy, "Christianity and Socialism," *Christian Socialist* (March 15, 1914), p. 42.

49. James P. Cannon's introduction to *Eugene V. Debs Speaks*, p. 28.

50. "Plea for Solidarity," Ibid., p. 206.

51. Ibid., p. 48.

52. *Edward Bellamy: Selected Writings on Religion and Society* (New York: The Liberal Arts Press, 1955), p. xxxiii.

53. "Religion of Solidarity," *Bellamy: Selected Writings*, p. 22.

54. Debs' speech at Girard, Kansas, May 23, 1908. From *Debs: His Writings and Speeches (Authorized)* (St. Louis: Phil Wagner, 1908), p. 475.

55. Ibid., p. 484.

56. Philip S. Foner, *The Industrial Workers of the World: 1905–1917* (New York: International Publishers, 1965), p. 23n.

57. Foner, *The Industrial Workers of the World*, p. 23n.

58. William Z. Foster, "Syndicalism in the United States," *The Communist* (July 1937), p. 1044. Quoted in Foner, p. 20.

59. Georges Sorel, *Reflections on Violence*, translated by T. E. Hulme and J. Roth (London: Collier-Macmillan, 1950), pp. 125–126.

60. John Graham Brooks, *Labor's Challenge to the Social Order: Democracy Its Own Critic and Educator* (New York: Macmillan, 1920), p. 376.

61. James Gilbert, *Designing the Industrial State: The Intellectual*

Pursuit of Collectivism in America, 1880–1940 (Chicago: Quadrangle Books, 1972), p. 54.

62. Sorel, p. 243.

63. Examples are numerous. Some samples can be found in various issues of the *IW* such as "What the Bible Says" February 12, 1910, p. 4; letter from "Abe R. Deen" January 4, 1912, p. 3; a poem entitled "The Proletaire" July 23, 1910, p. 2; and "A Call to Action" February 26, 1910, p. 2.

3

Wobbly Hymnody: The Music of Solidarity

The music of the I.W.W., perhaps more than any of the union's other weapons of struggle, served to "fan the flames of discontent," to generate the spirit of rebellion by which the Wobblies hoped to win the American working class to industrial unionism. Although singing has long been part of various movements for social change in American history, the singing unionism of the Industrial Workers of the World possessed a spirit of solidarity and class consciousness that made it unique. As an older soldier explains to a younger one in James Jones' 1952 novel of World War II, *From Here to Eternity*:

There has never been anything like them [the I.W.W.] before or since. They called themselves materialist-economists but what they really were was a religion. They were workstiffs and bindlebums like you and me, but they were welded together by a vision we don't possess. It was their vision that made them powerful. And sing! you never heard anyone sing the way these guys sung! Nobody sings like they did unless its for a religion.[1]

Indeed, one cannot ignore the striking parallel between the Wobblies' use of music and that of American Protestantism. The genre of hymnody, especially in those Gospel songs that were popularized in the 1870's through the efforts of Dwight L. Moody, the American evangelist, and his musical associate, Ira D. Sankey, provided the Wobblies with a good portion of its arsenal of parody to use against the "pie in the sky" attitudes of organized religion.[2] "They raided the hymnbook of Moody-and-Sankey revivalism,"[3] to arrive at such popular Wobbly "hymns" as "Hold the Fort" and "There is Power in a Union." The *Little Red Songbook* (hereafter abbreviated as *LRS*), in which these and many other Wobbly parodies and songs appeared was "what the hymnbook and the *Discipline of the Methodist Church* had been to the frontier preachers— the sum and touchstone of faith, the pearl of revelation, the coal of fire touching their lips with eloquence."[4]

The I.W.W. borrowed from American Protestantism not only the tunes of many of its hymns, but also the actual form of hymn-singing, camp meetings and revivalism, particularly in the Western part of the country. Before looking at specific songs of the Wobblies and examining their relationship to American hymnody, it may be useful to assess briefly how American Protestantism used gospel songs and folk hymns in its attempts to win souls—especially those of the disinherited—to its flock. (See Appendix II for tunes and lyrics of various hymns parodied by the Wobblies.)

In his well-known work, *The Social Sources of Denominationalism*, H. Richard Niebuhr refers to the Methodist revival as "the last great religious revolution of the disinherited in Christendom." He then proceeds to compare the social causes for the rise of socialist ideologies with those that "formed the background of religious revolutions in previous centuries" such as "the actual exclusion of the poor from churches grown emotionally too cold, ethically too neutral, intellectually too sober, socially too aristocratic to attract the men who suffered under the oppression of monotonous toil, of insufficient livelihood and the sense of social inferiority."[5] In America, the Methodist church became so closely associated, in the minds of many, with the westward movement that "no group . . . seemed more providentially designed to capitalize on the conditions of the advancing American frontier than the Methodists."[6]

Because of the lack of metropolitan and educational centers along the route of westward expansion, the so-called "frontier churches"—Methodists, Baptists, and small "fringe" sects— relied heavily on circuit riders and "fervently evangelical" camp meetings. In the frontier settlements, writes music scholar

William Jenson Reynolds, "the music used in the religious services consisted of folk and camp-meeting hymns and itinerant evangelists imported the gospel songs to these areas as they became popular in the East and Midwest."[7] Largely because of their popular and emotional quality, these gospel songs appealed greatly to the uneducated masses who populated the frontier. The American gospel hymn, writes John Spencer Curwen at the end of the nineteenth century, "is nothing if it is not emotional. It takes a simple phrase and repeats it over and over again. There is no reasoning, nor are the lines made heavy with introspection. 'Tell me the story simply, as to a little child.' The feelings are touched; the stiffest of us become children again."[8]

Just as the gospel songs of American Protestantism took on vital significance during the course of the country's expansion westward, the Wobblies' "hymns" of industrial unionism first achieved popularity when the I.W.W. began increasingly to adopt a Western character. It is certainly no coincidence that the committee designed to discuss the possibility of issuing the first songbook was set up by the I.W.W. in 1908, the very year that J. H. Walsh, national organizer for the West Coast, and his famous "Overall Brigade" came from Spokane to the Fourth Annual Convention in Chicago to change the whole face of the I.W.W., giving it a decidedly Western flavor.[9] It was a time when the union was in turmoil. The direct-actionists, represented by Vincent St. John and William Trautmann, were engaged in vigorous ideological warfare with the proponents of political action, most notably Daniel De Leon of the Socialist Labor Party.[10] Walsh's crusaders, who saw political activity as a luxury for enjoyment by the more settled industrial workers of the East, not the rootless migrant workers of the West, brought a clear message to the convention: end the nitpicking and start organizing the unorganized. A letter written by a Western Wobbly to the *IUB* in June of 1908 seems to illustrate the attitude of the majority of I.W.W. members of the Pacific Northwest:

I hope that you won't print any of that junk about De Leon . . . as the great majority of members don't belong to the S.L.P. and the continued harping about these things will do more harm than good. Tell them there is too much to do to bother with such small matters, and if they don't like it go to hell, or some other place. It costs more to be eternally getting out these petty charges than the whole bunch of political fanatics are worth. The I.W.W. has no political affiliation, and that settles it, and any more of this damn dope about De Leon or S.L.P. will be very obnoxious to me and to hundreds of others that are the life of the I.W.W.[11]

To the disenfranchised, rootless worker of the Northwest—that element celebrated as the backbone of the Wobblies by J. H. Walsh and condemned as the "slum proletariat" by De Leon[12]—propaganda songs were a more powerful weapon of class struggle than the ballot box. "The labor situation in the northwest is just as it has been for some months," writes Walsh to the *IUB*, "thousands of idle men are tramping the country looking for jobs, while harvest hands are working as cheap as 75 cents per day." The unemployment situation is so critical, says Walsh, "that many around the headquarters have little to do but . . . compose poetry and work up songs for old tunes."[13] Walsh then includes the lyrics to "Hallelujia, I'm a Bum," the popular "theme song" of the Western Wobbly, asserting that "although this may not be as scientifically revolutionary as some would like . . . it certainly has its psychological effect upon the poor wage slave that inhabits the proletarian part of the city. . . . "[14]

In both the Wobbly songs and the Sankey gospel hymns of the 1870's, simplicity of theme took priority over doctrinal purity. "Gospel hymnody," writes Robert M. Stevenson in *Patterns of Protestant Church Music*, "has been a plough digging up the hardened surfaces of pavemented minds." "Its very obviousness," he writes,

has been its strength. Where delicacy or dignity can make no impress, gospel hymns stand up triumphing. In an age when religion must at least win mass approval in order to survive, in an age when religion must at least win a majority vote from the electorate, gospel hymnody is inevitable. Sankey songs are true folk music of the people.[15]

The intention of the gospel song, then, as Stevenson percep-
tively observes, is to convey a simple point as directly as possible, to win "a majority vote" by appealing to the hearts, not
the intellects, of the common people. The circuit riders and
frontier preachers of the West realized that, in trying to reach
the masses outside of the sophisticated urban centers, one song
is worth a dozen sacred texts. Likewise, in comparing the use
of songs with propaganda pamphlets, Joe Hill, in one of his
prison letters, asserts that:

A pamphlet, no matter how good, is never read more than once, but
a song is learned by heart and repeated over and over; and I maintain that if a person can put a few cold, common sense facts into a
song, and dress them . . . up in a cloak of humor to take the dryness
off of them, he will succeed in reaching a great number of workers
who are too unintelligent or too indifferent to read a pamphlet or an
editorial in economic science.[16]

The similarity of gospel tunes and Wobbly songs in their
common purpose of developing group consciousness and co-
hesiveness is, perhaps, extremely obvious. Less obvious, however, is the "mixed style" characterizing both types of songs.
In *No Offense*, his book on civil religion, John Cuddihy presents several excerpts from well-known Protestant hymns to
illustrate their uniquely "plain" style, combining elements of
high and low, sacred and profane.[17]

Before looking at specific songs, a more clear idea of the "sacred" and "profane" features of I.W.W. music is necessary. While
Emile Durkheim defines the profane simply as the ordinary or
mundane[18]—much in the manner that Cuddihy talks about a
"decorum of imperfection" in Protestant hymnody[19]—the "profane" element of Wobbly songs exist in their barbed, often
"blasphemous" satirical flavor. In a letter on the power of satirical songs, James Wilson writes to his fellow Wobblies: "What
more powerful way to excite ridicule than a comic song? How
very useful to bring out the hollowness of the sham religion-
ists, with their sounding drum and doleful chants, while they
pick our pockets."[20] Perhaps the most striking example of this
appears in the well-known parody of "Onward Christian Sol-

diers." This song, "Christians at War" by John F. Kendrick, first appeared in the ninth edition of the *LRS*, 1913, and opens with this devastating stanza:

> Onward Christian soldiers! Duty's way is plain;
> Slay your Christian brothers, or by them be slain;
> Pulpiteers are spouting effervescent swill,
> God above is calling you to rob and rape and kill;
> All your acts are sanctified by the Lamb on high;
> If you love the Holy Ghost, go murder pray and die.

Because of its harsh language and supposedly anti-Christian sentiments, Kendrick's song was often used as evidence against the Wobblies in various trials. In Everett, Washington, for example, during the 1917 murder trial of Thomas H. Tracy and seventy-four other Wobblies following the "Everett Massacre" (see Chapter 5), the prosecution tried to use lyrics of "Christians at War" as evidence of the subversive, anti-religious nature of the I.W.W. In response to the charges, Wobbly leader James P. Thompson said during his April 3 testimony:

The song is a satire, a sort of an argument against Christians going to war. It says "Onward Christian Soldiers, duty's way is plain. Slay your Christian neighbors or by them be slain." Behind that—plainly showing—is a Christian idea; "Don't slay your neighbors." It is inconsistent for Christians to talk about slaying their neighbors. (*IW* 4/14/17, p. 1)

If one views Wobbly songs in the context of Durkheim's and Cuddihy's sense of the word "profane"—as approximately equivalent to "plain"—numerous interesting examples emerge. The Wobbly songwriters go beyond the "decorum of imperfection" that Cuddihy finds in H. H. Milman's Palm Sunday hymn ("in lowly pomp ride on to die") and W. C. Dix's Christmas hymn ("that manger rude and bare")[21] to what one Wobbly writer describes as "the morality of the belly need."[22] One vivid example of this is found in the first few stanzas of "The Lumberjack's Prayer," a 1920 Wobbly song written by "T-Bone Slim" to the tune of "Praise God from Whom All Blessings Flow," a Sankey gospel hymn:

I pray dear Lord for Jesus' sake,
Give us this day a t-bone steak.
Hallowed be thy Holy Name,
But don't forget to send the same.

Oh, hear my humble cry, O Lord,
And send us down some decent board,
Brown gravy and some German fried
With sliced tomatoes on the side.

Observe me on my bended legs,
I'm asking you for ham and eggs,
And if You havest custard pies,
I'd like, dear Lord, the largest size.[23]

Similarly, the song "Out in the Breadline," appearing first in the 1911 edition of the *LRS*, expresses clearly the "morality of the belly need." Parodying another Sankey gospel hymn, "Throw Out the Life Line."[24] The song begins with this stanza:

Out in the breadline, the fool and the knave;
Out in the breadline, the sucker and the slave;
Coffee and doughnuts now take all our cash,
We're on the bum and we're glad to get hash.[25]

The "sacred" element in I.W.W. songs is, needless to say, more problematical than the profane. The most obvious reason for this is that the term cannot be used in the conventional sense, as pertaining to the supernatural or holy, when applied to the Wobblies. Rather, the term "sacred" might more closely approach the interpretation J. Paul Williams suggests in his article "The Nature of Religion," where he argues that while all forms of religiosity adhere to a belief-attitude that an ultimate of some kind exists, a religion need not view the ultimate as supernatural, but only as something "of supreme importance" to the individual or the group or the "final reality which . . . affects man's life."[26] Or, to borrow a term (and book title) from Paul Tillich, the "sacred" quality of I.W.W. songs is equivalent to an "ultimate concern." It is a quality, the Wobblies felt, that could be found not in the "business unionism" of the "American Separation of Labor" but only in the hearts of brave rebels like those found in the I.W.W. As one writer put it in an article entitled "Our Songs" (*IW* 5/27/16, p. 2):

The A.F.L. with its over two million members has no songs, no poetry and prose. The I.W.W. has a vast wealth of both, rising out of the toil and anguish of the disinherited. Only those who feel strongly and greatly break into song. Music is created deep in the very essence of things, and if really great, cannot belong to the shallow or the conventional. Only great movements marking turning points in the history of humanity have produced great songs, appealing to the masses because they voice the inarticulate feelings and aspirations of the masses.

Ironically, if one considers again Cuddihy's analysis of the "plainness" and Puritan "good taste" of American Protestant hymnody, with its rejection of "triumphal demeanor" and "vulgar boasting," the I.W.W. songs come closer than the hymns to the earlier sense of the sacred, as evoking fear, awe and respect.[27] Richard Brazier, who came to Spokane from Northern Ontario in 1907 and was a member of the I.W.W. committee which collected and published the songs for the first *LRS* in 1909, argued passionately in 1908 that the *LRS* would serve well to "make the I.W.W. known and to propagate its ideas and principles." The early advocates of the songbook, Brazier recalled much later in a 1968 article in *Labor History*, "The Story of the I.W.W.'s 'Little Red Songbook,'" insisted that the songbook contains songs that

shall call to judgement our oppressors and the profit system that they have devised. Songs of battles, flaunted wealth and thread-bare morality to scorn . . . these songs will deal with every aspect of the workers' lives. They will bring hope to them and courage to wage the good fight. They will be songs sowing the seeds of discontent and rebellion. We want our songs to stir the workers into action, to awaken them from an apathy and complacency that has made them accept their servitude as though it had been divinely ordained. We are sure that the power of the song will exalt the spirit of Rebellion.[28]

For the early Wobbly advocates of the songbook, like J. H. Walsh whom Brazier calls the "Father of the Little Red Songbook,"[29] the function of music in the building of industrial unionism—and eventually a Commonwealth of Toil—was crucial. While the Puritan or American Protestant style rejects the triumphal, preferring instead the unostentatious, (such as the story of Christ's inconspicuous entry into Jerusalem on the back of an ass)[30] the Wobblies use the language of exaltation whenever alluding to the inevitable victory of the working class over capitalism. Just as the cartoons of the I.W.W. often depict the worker as a powerful giant, towering triumphantly over the diminutive capitalist, the songs of the Wobblies, in their efforts to "stir the workers into action" and generate "courage to wage the good fight," celebrate enthusiastically the proletarian victory that is to come.

A dramatic example of this triumphant note appears in the song "Hold the Fort." Originally a gospel tune written by Bliss in 1870 about an incident in the Civil War ("Union" referring to the North), it first appeared in the eighth edition of the *LRS* in 1914. Although the labor version of the song is not a Wobbly original—it was adopted first by the Knights of Labor and then the British Transport Workers in 1890[31]—its "sacred" celebration of labor's inevitable triumph illustrates why it became and remained a Wobbly favorite. A comparison of the chorus of the original Bliss version with the labor version of 1890 reveals an important difference. While the gospel version puts its faith for salvation in an individual—the figure of Jesus—the labor version puts its faith in the collective strength of the union. The chorus of the gospel song is:

"Hold the fort, for I am coming,"
Jesus signals still,
Wave the answer back to Heaven,
"By thy grace we will."[32]

The chorus of the labor version makes no reference to an individual savior, human or divine, but only to the strength of the Union:

Hold the fort for we are coming—
Union men, be strong.

Side by side we battle onward,
Victory will come.

While the Bliss song possesses the quality of struggle and
eventual triumph that appealed to the Knights of Labor and
British Transport Workers of the nineteenth century—and later
to the Wobblies in the twentieth—it also contains two elements detrimental to the development of class consciousness.
One, as already mentioned, was the focus on individual heroes or villains. Besides the reference to Jesus in the chorus,
the Bliss song contains the lines "see the mighty host advancing, Satan leading on," "in our leader's name we'll triumph over
every foe," and "Onward comes our Great Commander, cheer,
my Comrades, cheer." The labor version, however, uses only
the pronoun "we" as it urges: "Union men be strong," "Side by
side we battle onward," and finally, "By our union we shall
triumph."

The second element of the Bliss song detrimental to class
consciousness is the implied belief that human effort, without
Divine Intervention, is essentially useless. Before the "Great
Commander," Jesus Christ, comes to the fort "with glorious
banner waving," the Bliss song depicts "mighty men around
us falling, courage almost gone." In the labor version, however, there is no such despair in human efforts, only "our
numbers still increasing," and the triumphant realization that
"victory is nigh" and that "by our union we shall triumph."
Thus, the 1890 labor version of "Hold the Fort" meets the criteria that Richard Brazier says were essential to songs included in the *LRS*: it awakens workers from apathy and avoids
any note of despair.[33]

The thematic shift, then, from the Bliss gospel song of 1870
to the militant labor song of 1890 (adopted by the I.W.W. in
1914) consists of a movement from the individual to the collective, from a negative to a positive view of human effort. In
this shift, however, is a parallel movement from the spiritual
to the secular. While the original tone of triumph is maintained between 1870 and 1890, all religious references disap-
pear in the adaptation by the British Transport Workers. In

a still later labor version—written by Wobbly poet and editor
Ralph Chaplin and appearing in the fifteenth edition of the
LRS—the song undergoes what might be seen as a spiritual
transformation.

Ralph Chaplin, author of numerous Wobbly songs, including "Solidarity Forever" (which Philip Foner calls "the greatest song yet produced by American labor"[34]), wrote his version of "Hold the Fort" while serving a prison sentence between
1918 and 1919 for his anti-war activities. Aptly retitled "All
Hell Can't Stop Us," Chaplin's version contains a prophetic rage
not present in the earlier labor version. In Chaplin's version,
the listener is transported to Armageddon where the "final
battle rages" and "tyrants quake with fear" at the advance of
"a world-wide revolution."[35] While both the Bliss and the earlier labor version emphasize persevering in the face of battle,
holding the fort and eventually emerging victorious, Chaplin's
song—as can be seen by its chorus—settles for nothing short
of annihilation of the enemy:

> Scorn to take the crumbs they drop us,
> All is ours by right!
> Onward, men! All hell can't stop us!
> Crush the parasite.

Ironically, Chaplin has apparently borrowed more—at least
in terms of apocalyptic zeal—from the Bliss hymn than the 1890
labor version. Furthermore, he has also undoubtedly borrowed from the universal anthem of revolutionary labor, "The
Internationale," which appears regularly in the *LRS*, from the
first edition on. This song of the world revolutionary movement emerged out of the formation of the Paris Commune (First
International) of the 1870's. The words were written in 1871
by Eugene Pottier, as the French army was killing hundreds
of Parisian communards, and was set to music in 1889 by a
Belgian worker named Pierre Degeyter when a labor conference was convening to establish the Second Socialist and Labor International.[36] Below are the most obvious parallels between Chaplin's "All Hell Can't Stop Us" and "The
Internationale":

	"Internationale"	"All Hell Can't Stop Us"
(1)	"Tis the final Conflict"	"Now the final battle rages . . ."
(2)	"For justice thunders condemnation	"With a voice like angry thunder
	A Better world's in birth . . ."	Arise and claim your own . . ."
(3)	"We workers ask not for their [capitalists] favors . . ."	"Scorn to take the crumbs they drop us . . ."
(4)	"We have been naught/We shall be All"	"Labor shall be all . . ."

"The Internationale," according to Hungarian musicologist János Maróthy, derived its melody-type "from the world of the Bourgeois heroic-lyric hymn and march."[37] This observation, to a certain extent, provides a key to a clearer understanding of the relationship between Wobbly songs and the hymnody of American Protestantism and, more specifically, between the I.W.W. and its despised antagonist, the Salvation Army—particularly in terms of how both organizations made use of "sacred" music.

Maróthy, who studied aesthetics under Marxist philosopher Georg Lukacs,[38] seeks to illustrate the class origins of music types. In *Music and the Bourgeois, Music and the Proletarian*, he points out that "there are two characteristic genres which—owing to their increasingly generalizing ideas and propagandistic character—played a special part in transmitting bourgeois musicality to the proletariat . . . the march and the hymn or anthem." This connection can be explained, Maróthy asserts, partially by the fact that "even in the bourgeois movements, they had been endowed with a 'universally popular character', and in this way, they had absorbed certain proletarian elements."[39] This was certainly the case with the Bliss and Sankey gospel songs which appealed strongly—as Methodist circuit riders and other frontier preachers well knew—to the rootless masses in the West. The writers of these hymns,

H. Wiley Hitchcock points out in his introduction to *Gospel Hymns*:

cannily adopted the early revival hymns' infectious pattern of verse followed by a catchy, and usually thunderous refrain. To it they adapted the predictable, and thus easily singable, melodic contours and smooth simple harmony . . . a kind of religious pop art almost irresistible in its visceral appeal.[40]

Thus, when the I.W.W. songwriters selected what Maróthy would call the "bourgeois mode" of the hymn for a large number of their parodies, they were drawing upon a genre that was already well imbued with the popular, or "proletarian mode." A clear illustration of this can be found in the perceived function of music by the Salvation Army. This group, scornfully dubbed "the Starvation Army" by the Wobblies, used songs in much the same way as the I.W.W. Established in the 1870's in England, in a decade when the gospel songs of Sankey and Bliss were gaining popularity the Salvation Army sought and used songs that were composed in the language of the people.

In the first issue of the Army's songbook, *The Salvationist* (January 1879), the word "song" was substituted for the word "hymn" in an effort "at breaking the spell of dislike with which the masses had come to regard anything that was 'churchy'."[41] Also, purporting to take their cue from Martin Luther himself who declared that "the words of hymns should have a swing and a good strong metre," the Salvationists abandoned traditional hymn tunes for "popular melodies" and even "downright comic-song tunes."[42] Like the I.W.W., the Salvation Army sought to win converts among the largely uneducated masses, the proletariat whose musical tastes were shaped not by the Gregorian tradition but by ditties of the barroom and music hall.

The I.W.W. and the Salvation Army were, in effect, competing for the same audience, for the same souls. The "Army succeeded in a way that the traditional churches did not in attracting the support of the foot-loose elements," that same element from which the Wobblies wished to recruit. Furthermore, the methods employed by the Army were those methods which the Wobblies were to imitate, particularly in the West.

"Street preaching was revived as a regular feature," writes S. D. Clark about the Salvation Army.

and the combination of street preaching with parades led by brass bands provided an effective means of attracting attention. Crowds were gathered together on street corners, in public parks and other open spaces, and when a sufficient state of religious enthusiasm had been aroused, the parade was paraded to the barracks where the revivalist meeting took place.[43]

Although Clark is speaking largely about the Army as a sect functioning in Canada, the comments apply to the activities of the Army everywhere. And in his assessment of the class allegiance of the Salvation Army, one almost hears the voice of the I.W.W. as it derides the "Starvation Army" for distracting the working class by feeding them "religious dope" instead of organizing them to fight against the ruling rich. "In the long run, perhaps," writes Clark,

the effect of the influence of such a movement as the Salvation Army was to arrest the development of a stable urban order. Peoples' attentions were diverted from the real problems of an industrial society; the Army following tended to be held in a state of political and economic illiteracy. The effect was particularly evident in retarding the development of working class organizations.[44]

Consequently, hostility toward the Salvation Army appears in much of the I.W.W.'s music, cartoons, and journalism. This feeling, no doubt, was mutual since both groups competed for the same audience. "The Salvation Army is somewhat hostile to our movement," writes a Wobbly from Minneapolis, "the captain of the holy host tries to keep the crowds away, telling them to come to their hall and to keep away from the devils— meaning us. But in spite of the sky pilots and their big drums, we manage to get the best crowds."[45] In a similar spirit of hostile competition, Richard Brazier gleefully recalls how the Wobblies "at times would sing note by note with the Salvation Army at our street meetings, only their words were describing Heaven above, and our Hell right here—to the same tune."[46]

If the I.W.W., as Brazier contends, does "not object to religious bodies, as such,"[47] why does it devote so much energy
and wrath opposing the Salvation Army? Why is this the group,
the only specific religious organization, singled out for ridicule
in Joe Hill's parodies? To answer these questions—before
looking specifically at Hill and his hymn parodies—it is useful
to refer back to a remark of Father Hagerty's mentioned in
the previous chapter. "Religion has no more to do with socialism," Hagerty states, "than it has with meat and bread. . . .
It is wholly beyond the scope of the Church's mission to deal
with questions of social economy."[48] In the eyes of the Wobblies, the Salvation Army functioned as an economic organization as well as a religious one and it is on the economic level
that it poses a threat to the working class. In a 1910 issue of
the *IW*, for example, the editor, after accusing the Army of being
"always the staunch supporter of the capitalist," writes the
following about the Salvation Army:

In the name of Jesus, they strenuously support the most vicious
practices of the most vicious age. They teach contentment with small
means or no means at all—while they never leave unturned a stone
that may cover a rusty nickel. They are vultures in the form of hu-
mans. They are the personification of all that is degenerate in a land
and age of degeneracy. They beg pennies, clothing and furniture in
the name of Christ and supposedly to 'feed and clothe his lambs,' but
in reality to sell their things to those who are too poor to buy them
from a store.[49]

The chief crime, then, of which the Wobblies accuse the Army
is an economic one. While gaining the large percentage of its
support—as do most sects—"from that section of the population which has lost a sense of belonging to any settled society," from the "socially unattached" or "footloose"[50]—the Army
victimizes rather than helps (or organizes) the working class.
For this reason, the working class, long before the formation
of the I.W.W. in 1905, was often hostile to the Salvation Army.
In writing of the Army's history between 1878 and 1886, for
example, Salvationist Robert Sandall says, in the second of five
volumes of *The History of the Salvation Army*:

Apart from the occasions of actual opposition, roughs seldom or never sang the original words. When they were attacking Salvationists and trying to sing them down they would sometimes roar out parodies.[51]

Likewise, in the United States, Wobbly songwriters used the weapon of parody to wage war against the Salvationists, particularly in the free-speech fights of Western America. The attacks were now, however, one-sided, for the Army itself, along with the Volunteers of America, "delighted in trying to break up the I.W.W. street meetings with blare of trumpets, and banging of drum." But, as J. H. Walsh was fond of boasting, "we have as many tunes and songs as they have hymns; and while we may borrow a hymn tune from them, we will use our own words. If they do not quiet down a little we will add some bagpipes to the band, and that will quiet them."[52] Using the methods, tactics and cultural conventions of the enemy class and its allies[53] is an important part of the I.W.W.'s efforts, as the Preamble proclaims, toward "forming the new society within the shell of the old." "The form of industrial unionism," observed one Wobbly writer in the *IW* (3/1/12, p. 3) "must be in conformity with that of capitalist production, it must organize cell for cell, tissue for tissue with capitalism." Just as the I.W.W. carefully observed industrial development in America, often consciously duplicating the tactics of American capitalism for the advancement of the proletarian cause, Wobbly song writers, who "had learned most of their hymns at street missions and from their contacts with the Salvation Army,"[54] observed American religion.

In the famous Western free-speech fights, this was particularly evident. These fights, which numbered about twenty between 1909 and 1913, all involved the right of the I.W.W. to recruit members at street meetings.[55] The most widely celebrated of these struggles occurred in Spokane, Washington, in 1909–10; Fresno, California, in 1910–11; and San Diego in 1912. The pattern for these and other battles was similar: in opposition to city ordinances that forbade "soapboxers" from speaking on public street corners, Wobbly speakers would defy the law by mounting the soapboxes, addressing the crowd of "fellow workers and friends," and allowing themselves, one by one, to be dragged off to jail by the authorities. "Whenever any local union becomes involved in a free speech fight," Vincent St. John explained to a *New York Times* reporter, "they notify the general office and that information is sent to all local unions . . . with the request that if they have any members that are footloose to send them along."[56] Often, as jails began to fill beyond their capacities and public sentiment began to grow for workers who were deprived of their First Amendment rights, city authorities began to reconsider the oppressive ordinances. The overall value and purpose of these fights is perhaps summed up best by Melvyn Dubofsky:

For Wobblies free-speech fights involved nothing so abstract as defending the Constitution, preserving the Bill of Rights, or protecting the civil liberties of American citizens. They were instigated primarily to overcome resistance to I.W.W. organizing tactics and also to demonstrate that America's dispossessed could, through direct action, challenge established authority.[57]

The songs of Joe Hill played an important role in launching this challenge. Although evidence is scant about whether this famous Wobbly songwriter and martyr actually participated in free-speech fights,[58] his songs undoubtedly had an impact. Since many of the anti–street-speaking ordinances in the West exempted the Salvation Army and other religious groups from the ban, it is not surprising that Joe Hill and other Wobblies saw the religious groups as serving as agents of the capitalists in denying them the right to organize, the right to counterpose their union to the "job sharks" who sold employment to the workers in Spokane and elsewhere.

When the I.W.W. recruitment campaign attempted to bypass the job sharks, write two contemporary Wobblies, Dean Nolan and Fred Thompson, "these employment agents countered by getting the Salvation Army or other religious groups to drown out the I.W.W. speakers with trumpet and drum."[59] Joe Hill, it can be argued, was vigorously protesting this complicity of organized religion with oppressive, anti–working-class forces, rather than religion itself. In fact, as Thompson points out in a booklet entitled *Joe Hill*, "Hill's boyhood had been spent in a religious family that held to a religious code. He dropped his theology, it would seem, but not the value system that went with it."[60]

In two of Hill's most popular parodies, "There is Power in a Union" and "The Preacher and the Slave," one finds this duality operating: opposition to conventional theology, especially when it takes a pro-capitalist economic form, and alignment with an essentially Christian value system.

"The Preacher and the Slave," perhaps Hill's best-loved song, was written in 1911 to the tune of "In the Sweet Bye and Bye," a Salvation Army favorite. The main chorus, which introduced the expression "pie-in-the-sky" into the American vernacular, illustrates the reply that "long-haired preachers" make "when asked about something to eat" by hungry workers:

> You will eat, bye and bye,
> In that glorious land above the sky;
> Work and pray, live on hay,
> You'll get pie in the sky when you die.[61]

The second and third verses, after introducing the "long-haired preachers [who] come out every night" in the first, proceed to illustrate the economic message, shrouded in religious rhetoric, that the Wobblies ridicule:

> And the starvation army they play,
> And they sing and they clap and they pray,
> Till they get all your coin on the drum,
> Then they tell you when you are on the bum.
> (Chorus)

> If you fight hard for children and wife—
> Try to get something good in this life—
> You're a sinner and bad man, they tell,
> When you die you will sure go to hell.
> (Chorus)

In response to this theology of capitalism, the song urges that "workingmen of all countries unite," fighting side by side until "the world and its wealth we have gained."

A year later, in the 1912 edition of the *LRS*, Joe Hill inverts the theology in "Casey Jones—the Union Scab." Casey Jones, an engineer on the Southern Pacific line, refuses to go along with a strike, insisting that he must keep "his junk pile running." When he is killed as the train runs off the track, Casey is welcomed into heaven by "Boss" St. Peter who hires him to scab on the angels, but "Angel Union No. 23 . . . promptly fired Casey down the Golden Stair." His fate is one well deserved by a scab, according to I.W.W. "theology":

> Casey Jones went to Hell a-flying;
> "Casey Jones," the Devil said, "oh fine,
> Casey Jones, get busy shoveling sulpher—
> That's what you get for scabbing on the S.P. line."[62]

In "There is Power in a Union," which first appeared in the 1913 edition of the *LRS*, Hill celebrates, in triumphant terms, the good that can come if workers "join in the grand Industrial band." Written to the tune of "There is Power in the Blood," another Salvation Army favorite, this song again illustrates the contrast between empty theological rhetoric and Hill's conception of the genuine Christian values of brotherhood and solidarity. The chorus, as militantly exuberant as any in labor music, proclaims,

> There is pow'r, there is pow'r
> In a band of workingmen,
> When they stand hand in hand,
> That's a pow'r, that's a pow'r
> That must rule in every land—
> One Industrial Union grand.

The first three stanzas in this song demonstrate, perhaps better than any others among Hill's many songs, the contradiction which the Wobblies saw between the "mansions of gold" theology of conservative Christianity and the "eggs and ham," economic realities facing the working class:

> Would you have freedom from wage slavery,
> Then join in the grand Industrial band;

Would you from mis'ry and hunger be free,
Then come, do your share, like a man.
(Chorus)

Would you have mansions of gold in the sky.
And live in a shack, way in the back?
Would you have wings up in heaven to fly,
And starve here with rage on your back?

If you've had 'nuf of the "blood of the lamb"
Then join in the grand Industrial band,
If, for a change, you would have eggs and ham,
Then come, do you share, like a man.[63]

In discussing the transformation of "bourgeois music," such
as marches and hymns, into genuine proletarian forms, "bourgeois illusions cannot survive for a single day if they are con-
fronted with the reality of life as sensed by the proletariat."[64]
Whether one accepts or rejects this Marxist assessment of
Maróthy, it is clear that the I.W.W., in its use of the Protestant hymn, was attempting (often successfully) to reveal the
plight of the working class to middle-class America. It was also
attempting to tap the energy of Moody revivalism to win rootless, disinherited workers—particularly Western workers—to
the cause of revolutionary industrial unionism.

An advertisement for the *Little Red Songbook*, appearing in
a 1912 issue of the *IW*, stresses the "sacred" nature of these
rousing, revolutionary songs in their opposition to "profane"
industrial capitalism. The advertisement, spiritually triumphant in its language, reads as follows:

SONGS! SONGS!
To fan the flames of discontent
Songs of Joy!
Songs of Sorrow!
Songs of Sarcasm!
Songs of the MISERIES THAT ARE
Songs of the Happiness to Be
Songs that strip Capitalism bare;
Show the shams of Civilization;
mock the masters' moral;

scorn the smug respectability
of the satisfied class; and
drown in one glad burst of
passion the profit patriotism
of the Plunderbund![65]

NOTES

1. James Jones, *From Here to Eternity* (New York: Charles Scribner's Sons, 1952), p. 640.

2. William Jensen Reynolds, *A Survey of Christian Hymnody* (New York: Holt, Rinehart and Winston, 1963), pp. 74–75 and 103.

3. Bernard A. Weisberger, "Here Come the Wobblies," reprinted in *American Vistas: 1877 to the Present*, ed. Leonard Dinnerstein and Kenneth T. Jackson (New York: Oxford University Press, 1971), p. 109.

4. Ibid., p. 108.

5. H. Richard Niebuhr, *The Social Sources of Denominationalism* (Cleveland and New York: Meridan Books, 1929), pp. 72–73.

6. Sidney E. Ahlstrom, *A Religious History of the American People* (New Haven and London: Yale University Press, 1972), p. 436.

7. Reynolds, p. 103.

8. John Spencer Curwen, *Studies in the Worship Music* (London: J. Curwen and Sons, 1885), p. 40.

9. Weisberger, p. 108.

10. Philip S. Foner, *The Industrial Workers of the World: 1905–1917* (New York: International Publishers, 1965), p. 106.

11. *Industrial Union Bulletin*, June 27, 1908, p. 2.

12. Ibid., February 27, 1909, p. 2.

13. Ibid., September 5, 1908 and April 4, 1908, pp. 1, 2.

14. Ibid., April 4, 1908, p. 2.

15. Robert M. Stevenson, *Patterns of Protestant Church Music* (Durham, North Carolina: Duke University Press, 1953), p. 162.

16. Philip S. Foner, ed., *The Letters of Joe Hill* (New York: Oak Publications, 1965), p. 16.

17. John Murray Cuddihy, *No Offense: Civil Religion and Protestant Taste* (New York: Seabury Press, 1978), pp. 200–201.

18. Emile Durkheim, *The Elementary Forms of the Religious Life*, trans. Joseph Ward Swain (New York: Collier, 1961), p. 52.

19. Cuddihy's subtitle for Chapter 8 of *No Offense* in which he discusses the "mixed style" of Protestantism and the requirement, on the part of American Puritanism, that "religious bodies exchange a triumphal demeanor for the civil demeanor of the denomination." (p. 191).

20. *IUB*, July 25, 1908, p. 1.

21. Cuddihy, pp. 200–201.

22. *IW*, May 28, 1910, p. 2.

23. I.W.W., *Songs of the Workers: To Fan the Flames of Discontent*, 34th edition (Chicago: Industrial Workers of the World, May 1, 1973), p. 50. First appeared in the 17th edition. The "Doxology," upon which the T-Bone Slim song is based, appears as Hymn #3 in Sankey's *Gospel Hymns*, originally published in 1895 and reprinted by Da Capo Press in 1972.

24. Ira D. Sankey, et al., *Gospel Hymns: Nos. 1 to 6 Complete* (New York: Da Capo Press, 1972), p. 625, hymn #615.

25. *Songs of the Workers*, p. 61. First appeared in the third edition of the songbook in 1910.

26. J. Paul Williams, "The Nature of Religion," *Journal for the Scientific Study of Religion* 2, 1(October 1962), p. 8.

27. Ronald L. Johnstone, *Religion and Society in Interaction* (Englewood Cliffs, New Jersey: Prentice-Hall, 1975), p. 17.

28. Richard Brazier, "The Story of the I.W.W.'s 'Little Red Songbook,' " *Labor History* II, 1(Winter 1968), p. 97.

29. Ibid., p. 95.

30. Cuddihy, p. 199.

31. *Songs of the Workers*, p. 33.

32. "In 1870, at a Sunday School convention, Philip P. Bliss, song leader for the convention and composer of several Civil War ballads, wrote 'Hold the Fort' in commemoration of General Sherman's successful effort, with a small number of Union soldiers, to 'hold the fort' against the Confederate troops' effort to destroy a small fort and the supplies therein in October of 1864." From *Reader's Digest Family Song Book of Faith and Joy*, edited by William L. Simon (Pleasantville, New York: Reader's Digest Assoc., 1975), p. 139.

33. Sankey, et al., *Gospel Hymns*, p. 7, hymn #11.

34. Brazier, p. 97.

35. Foner, *Industrial Workers of the World*, p. 155.

36. *Songs of the Workers*, p. 43. First appeared in 15th edition, 1919.

37. János Márothy, *Music and the Bourgeois, Music and the Proletarian* (Akademiai Kiado: Budapest, 1974), p. 445.

38. Ernest Kay, ed., *International Who's Who in Music and Musician's Directory*, 7th ed. (Cambridge: Cambridge University Press, 1975), p. 590.

39. Márothy, pp. 414–415.

40. Hitchcock's introduction to *Gospel Hymns: Nos. 1–6 Complete*.

41. Robert Sandall, *The History of the Salvation Army* (V. II 1878–1886) (London: Thomas Nelson and Sons, 1950), p. 107.

42. Ibid., pp. 111 and 109.

43. S. D. Clark, *Church and Sect in Canada* (Toronto: University of Toronto Press, 1948), p. 419.

44. Ibid., p. 424.

45. *IW*, April 16, 1910, p. 3.

46. Brazier, p. 99.

47. Ibid., p. 94.

48. *International Socialist Review* (October 1902), p. 229.

49. "Jesus(?)", *IW*, October 8, 1910, p. 2.

50. Clark, p. 433.

51. Robert Sandall, *The History of the Salvation Army* (V. II 1878–1886) (London: Thomas Nelson and Sons, 1950), p. 111.

52. Brazier, p. 94.

53. As an editorial in the January 18, 1912, issue of *Industrial Worker* points out, the Wobblies believed strongly that the Salvation Army, often exempt from "street rally laws" used to imprison I.W.W. members, was "the ally of the master class." (p. 2).

54. Foner, *I.W.W.*, p. 153.

55. Joyce L. Kornbluh, *Rebel Voices: An I.W.W. Anthology* (Ann Arbor: University of Michigan Press, 1968), p. 95.

56. The *New York Times*, May 9, 1912.

57. Melvyn Dubofsky, *We Shall Be All: A History of the I.W.W.* (New York: Quadrangle Press, 1969), p. 173.

58. Dean Nolan and Fred Thompson, in their pamphlet, *Joe Hill: I.W.W. Songwriter* (Chicago: I.W.W., 1979), are not convinced that Hill spoke, was arrested, or even appeared at any of the free-speech battles (pp. 8–9).

59. Ibid., p. 7.

60. Fred Thompson, *Joe Hill* (San Diego: Fanshen Printing Collective, 1971), p. 17.

61. "The Preacher and the Slave," *Songs of the Workers*, p. 64.

62. Ibid., p. 60.

63. "There is Power in a Union," *Songs of the Workers*, p. 8. This song, as well as "Stung Right" and "The Preacher and the Slave," was sung by "fellow workers" at the memorial service for Joe Hill held in Chicago on November 25, 1915. The funeral program is included in the Joe Hill file at the Labadie Collection at the University of Michigan and is included by Joyce Kornbluh in *Rebel Voices*, pp. 152–153.

64. Márothy, p. 429.

65. *IW*, July 11, 1912, p. 4.

4

The Religious Question in the Wobbly Press

"The Wobblies had a compulsion to publish newspapers," writes Joseph R. Conlin, "and a positive knack for the craft." Indeed, one partial bibliography attributes sixty-six periodical publications to the I.W.W. between 1905 and 1919.[1] Their newspapers, like their songbooks, provided the Wobblies with a relatively inexpensive means of reaching the masses with the gospel of industrial unionism. When capitalism is eventually overthrown, the I.W.W. believed, it would be the educated industrial unionist that would lead the working class toward the Cooperative Commonwealth.[2] Unlike the songs, which were always triumphant, always animated with the pure spirit of rebellion, I.W.W. journalism mixed polemics with its rebellion. Whether on the picket line or in the pages of its press, the Wobblies always enjoyed a good fight, and the *Industrial Worker, Solidarity*, the *Industrial Union Bulletin* and other Wobbly newspapers virtually bristled with debate. While certainly partial to controversies regarding radical theory and class warfare strategies, the I.W.W. press tackled almost any subject that engaged the interest of working men and women, including the "religious question."

An examination of the treatment of religion in the I.W.W. press makes several points very clear. First, that most historians writing about the Progressive Era, such as Henry May in *The End of American Innocence*, go too far when they charge that the I.W.W. was prepared to see religion "thrown on the

ash heap" along with patriotism and "pussy-footing legal-
ism."[3] Rather, as Father Hagerty early asserted and the journalism clearly illustrates, the majority of Wobblies seemed to
view religion, at least as it relates to personal faith, as a private matter having little or nothing to do with the economic
realities of capitalist society.

Secondly, the character of Jesus plays an important role in
the I.W.W. press, appearing variously as a hobo, a rebel, a socialist, and a proletarian—carpenter by trade—who stood up
for and eventually died while defending the rights of the
working class. The figure of Jesus is often contrasted with the
persons and organizations which represent, in the eyes of the
I.W.W., the voices of hypocrisy—such as Billy Sunday, the
"Starvation Army" and the Y.M.C.A.—rather than the true
spirit of Christianity.

Thirdly, the I.W.W. press, especially as the United States
moved closer toward involvement in the Great European War,
often contrasted the peaceful values of "pure" Christianity with
the bloody reality of American militarism. World War I, for the
militants of the I.W.W., represented world capitalism's brutal
quest for new markets for which the working class was being
used as cannon fodder to defend the wealthy. "General Sherman said: 'War is hell,' " writes Wobbly editor Walker C. Smith,
"Don't go to Hell in order to give the capitalists a bigger slice
of heaven."[4] It was around the issue of the war, perhaps more
than any other concern of the Wobbly press, that the I.W.W.
consolidated most articulately its rhetorical arsenal in opposition to Christian hypocrisy. "Christians at War" became the
anthem of the anti-militarist rebels of the Industrial Workers
of the World.

Finally, the I.W.W. press occasionally draws a direct parallel between the Wobblies and a religion or church. Such an
equation, it must be quickly added, occurs infrequently.
Throughout this work, I have attempted to avoid the reductionist fallacy which has emerged, among other places, in the
fiction of Wallace Stegner and James Jones. When the I.W.W.
itself adopts this pattern, however, it does so usually for the
sake of expediency, challenging the government to abide by its
constitutional guarantee of freedom of religion. The I.W.W., the

argument usually runs, is itself a religion for the working class and, thus, cannot be interfered with by either government or business. To allow traditional religious organizations like the Salvation Army access to street corners while denying the same right to the I.W.W., say the Wobbly polemicists, is clearly unconstitutional. Also, on a less expedient and more philosophical level, some Wobbly writers, such as Covington Hall, argue that the American working class will accomplish nothing if it fails to "center around some great ideal, some sublime, heart-stirring conception of the 'world as it ought to be.' "[5]

The I.W.W., like the Finnish Socialist Federation to be considered in another chapter, believed that religion should be treated as a private matter, not as an institutional structure for social control. When the latter is substituted for the former, the Wobblies believed, the results are often destructive to the interests of the working class. In the first issue of the *Industrial Worker*, published in Spokane, the editors inform their readers that the newspaper "will be devoted entirely to upholding the interests of the working class, with the understanding that those who do useful work are the only class in society who have the moral or ethical right to an existence." Elsewhere in the opening editorial of this "curtain raiser" issue, the editors state:

Various papers have been and are printed in Spokane pretending to uphold the workers' interests—some of them political and some of them religious in nature, and we would state to begin with that we are not a religious organization and so neither are we an anti-religious body. We do not quarrel with any man's religious convictions—we have our hands full trying to make a living in this world and those that have settled that problem for themselves may have time to look to the BURNING question of the hereafter.[6]

Most of the Wobblies no doubt accepted the spirit of Father Hagerty's sharp distinction between economic and religious issues, while nevertheless often relying on scriptural messages to make revolutionary economic points. In the July 1, 1909, issue of the *IW*, for example, a writer strongly asserts that "the I.W.W. is an economic organization [dealing] with the bread-and-butter questions in this world." But then the writer, pursuing a Biblical path, continues:

The first economic thought in the Lord's Prayer is "give us this day our daily bread." Whether or not a man has an immortal soul, he at least has a body. To exist as a man in the world he must have his daily bread. It is the purpose of the I.W.W. to get the daily bread for the workers, and also all the good things of life. In the new "Jerusalem," some may hope that there will be no employing class.[7]

The question of private religious affiliation or creed, then, is of secondary importance to the reality of the class struggle, to the "daily bread" which workers must all fight to acquire. In a 1916 article entitled "Our Attitude Toward Religion," Albert B. Prashner expresses an opinion that seems to reflect the attitude of the I.W.W. as a whole:

It makes no difference to the wage-worker whether the employer is Jew, Christian, or atheist. The same thing applies to the worker alongside of us on the job. When the worker becomes conscious of the class to which he belongs and that his interests are identical with his class, his particular creed cannot hold him back anymore than driftwood can hold back the tide. I would rather have a fighting Irish Catholic by my side in a strike than any spineless "intellectual dilettante."[8]

The I.W.W. was neither bent on tossing religion "on the ash heap," as May contends, nor was it entirely anti-religious as most historians believed. Indeed, one Wobbly unionist, in writing to the *IW* in 1910 about the need for "a work embodying the principles of Industrial Unionism in general and the I.W.W. in particular," emphasizes that one of the topics covered should be "the attitude of the I.W.W. toward religion."[9] It is important to realize, however, that the I.W.W., while respecting the "private" religious conviction of each Fellow Worker, insisted on the right to submit religion to the test of "public" discourse and debate. In a column entitled "Proletarian Thoughts," George M. Falconer strongly asserts the following:

Religion is no more a private matter than is politics. If religion is altogether good it is in no danger from discussion or criticism. If it, in any way, hinders mental or moral progress or tends to block the march of evolution, it should be scrapped like any other useless antique. "There can be no alleviation for the suffering of mankind," says Professor Huxley, "except in absolute veracity of thought and action and in a resolute facing of the world as it is, with all garments thrown off." The big crime of today is the smug hypocrisy of self-deception.[10]

It is the "smug hypocrisy of self-deception" that irked the I.W.W. most about the form religion often takes in capitalist America. Discussions in the I.W.W. newspapers generally view religion not as an inherently negative thing, but as a matter to be pondered by the individual worker, subject always to open discourse in the press of the revolutionary union.

In order to clarify the next two areas of religious discussion found in I.W.W. newspapers—the character of Jesus as a foil to pseudo-Christian persons and organizations and the Wobbly critique (in religious terms) of American militarism—it is helpful to evaluate two concepts that have played an influential, if not controversial, role in American religious life: millennialism and civil religion. Taken together, these concepts provide a theoretical context in which to examine the role of religion in the I.W.W. press generally and, more specifically, the I.W.W.'s characterization of the historical and mythical Jesus, and its opposition to World War I.

In drawing his parallel between the I.W.W. and "primitive millennarianism,"[11] Melvyn Dubofsky, in *We Shall Be All*, does not go far enough. Quoting from E. J. Hobsbawm's influential 1959 book, *Primitive Rebels*, Dubofsky states that the I.W.W. shares with the "millennarians" the "hope of a complete and radical change in the world which will be reflected in the millennium, a world shorn of all its present deficiencies."[12] Unlike the Marxists, Dubofsky continues, the I.W.W. "never abandoned primitive millennarian dreams of a final conflict, a Judgement Day when the exploiters would be turned out and the banner of Industrial Freedom raised over the workshops of the world. . . . "[13] This analogy, while pertinent as far as it goes, makes no qualitative addition to Hobsbawm's earlier text which asserts that this radical millennialism is present, almost by definition, "in all revolutionary movements of whatever kind. . . ."[14]

In order to see beyond this fairly obvious parallel between the I.W.W. and millennialist vision, both of which anticipated an overturning of the present, corrupt order, it is useful to view the ideas of some modern Christian scholars in connection with I.W.W. journalism. "Between the two extremes of the 'pure' millennarian and the 'pure' political revolutionary," writes Hobsbawm, "all manner of intermediate positions are possible."[15] Dubofsky, in focusing on the latter extreme, depicts an I.W.W. that exemplifies only the secular mode, while theologian Paul Tillich, in addressing the millennialism that comes closer to Hobsbawm's "pure" category, speaks of the "cosmic struggle" seen by early Christians, in which "there is one struggle and one end, the thousand year reign—that is, that which is beyond all history."[16] It is the sense of a struggle beyond history that characterizes millennialism—a battle that rages beyond the boundaries of space and time. In "the proletarian movements," Tillich continues, "we discover a unity that extends over the whole world . . . and the utopia of the classless society that lies before us."[17]

The proletarian nature of the I.W.W.'s vision is crucial. This quality is not unique to a revolutionary movement, however, since, as sociologist Roland Robertson observes, almost all messianic and millennialist cults are characterized by a state of being marginal and deprived, outside the mainstream economic world occupied by religious denominations.[18] For the I.W.W., it is the disinherited class, the proletariat, to which the future belongs. This class, according to Wobbly history, earned its place at the pinnacle of human evolution by its precapitalist appearance in the scheme of things. "Labor existed and was of value long before capital emerged from the womb of time," writes the quasi-mystical Wobbly poet-editor Covington Hall, "Labor was labor when Adam and Eve gathered fruits in the Garden of Eden.[19]

The Wobbly brand of millennialism, besides being unflinchingly proletarian, is also internationalist, universalist, and strongly rooted in the belief in a class struggle that has existed since the beginning of time. Like such social gospel activists as Walter Rauschenbusch and unlike the nineteenth century evangelicals, the Wobblies held that "the Kingdom would soon come in history in near if not full completeness, and it would come largely through the efforts of men."[20] Also like the social Christians, particularly Rauschenbusch, the Wobbly press often magnified the character of Jesus, claiming him as one of their own, in their vigorous opposition to the trappings of institutional religion. For the I.W.W., Jesus—"a proletaire, a Nazarene, the carpenter"—is the true proletarian rebel "whose words made systems, states and empires turn to dust."[21]

Dubofsky's parallel between the Wobbly and millennial visions—especially when seen in the context of such passages as the one just quoted—seems very sound, even occasionally obvious. Furthermore, if one adds the elements of internationalism or universality to the proletarian character of most millennialist movements, one could make a convincing case for a kind of Wobbly Millennialism.

A corollary to the I.W.W.'s participation in a kind of proletarian millennialism is the union's vigorous opposition to American civil religion. This term, dating back to Rousseau's *The Social Contract*, but finding a new application in Robert N. Bellah's 1967 essay, "Civil Religion in America," provides a framework for understanding the I.W.W.'s "anti-religion" reputation. The concept, in brief, holds that there have been two types of religion operating in American society, particular and general. The particular, of course, refers to that element of religion that is linked to specific churches or denominations. The general religion, according to Russell E. Richey and Donald G. Jones, in the introductory essay to their 1974 collection, *American Civil Religion*, "has been discussed under such categories as democratic faith, societal religion, the American Way, generalized religion, common faith, American Shinto, and now 'civil religion.'"[22] The crux of the position, as stated by Bellah, is that "there actually exists alongside of and rather clearly differentiated from the churches an elaborate and well-institutionalized civil religion in America,"[23] possessing its own set of rituals, sacred events, beliefs and symbols.

Many critics of this concept charge that its proponents and their conceptual models—Sidney Mead's "religion of the Republic," Will Herberg's "American Way of Life," W. Lloyd Warner's "Yankee City," etc.—all fall into a kind of religious nationalism, making the State an object of adoration and glorification.[24] Also, as Martin E. Marty and Herbert Richardson argue in their essays (in the Richey and Jones anthology), the term "civil religion" is an exclusionary one, concentrating on the cultural lives of Americans of European stock and ignoring Blacks, Chicanos, American Indians, and the foreign-born.[25] Although not using the term "civil religion," the Wobblies were always vehemently critical of that brand of civic piety that excludes working people, of any race, from the ranks of "the chosen"; and that tries to convince workers that it is their Christian, patriotic duty to do the bidding of the nation's "leaders": industrialists and politicians. Returning again to the song "Christians at War," one finds writer Kendrick's barbs aimed not so much at Christianity *per se*, but at Christianity in service to the capitalist state, in bloody obsequiousness to the "nation with the soul of a church."[26] In the last stanza of the song, for example, the writer reaches a peak of contempt for the butcherous deeds performed by a state which believes, as the third stanza declares, that "Christ okays the bill" and that everything is justified:

> Onward Christian soldiers! Blighting all you meet;
> Trample human freedom under pious feet.
> Praise the Lord whose dollar sign dupes his favored race!
> Make the foreign trash respect your bullion brand of grace.
> Trust in mock salvation, serve as tyrant's tools:
> History will say to you: "That pack of G . . . d . . . fools."[27]

The obvious reference, in lines three and four, to the clash between the "favored race" (White Americans) and the "foreign trash" (everyone else) points squarely at the Wobbly critique of American civil religion.

If the I.W.W. felt contempt for both organized, churchly religion and the smug piety of civil religion, they expressed unchecked scorn for the State and all its various servants. And often the rebellious spirit of Jesus, as it appears in Wobbly newspapers, stands in dramatic contrast to these institutional extensions of the capitalist system. If the term "civil" in civil religion is interpreted as John Murray Cuddihy has done in the title of his recent book—as giving "no offense"[28]—then Jesus, as the Wobblies viewed him, would have no place in a civil religion.

An article in the Nome *Industrial Journal*, comparing the "abuse and misrepresentation" the I.W.W. has experienced at "the hands of the capitalists and their labor fakirs" with the agony suffered by Christ, says:

Even the Nazarene was denounced as a disturber and an enemy of the State and of the established order of things, and to satisfy the desires of the profit-mongers and the political tyrants he was crucified. But from the persecution of those who cried 'crucify him' sprang the organized Christian church.

Such persecution, the writer continues, not only failed to put down Jesus and his followers, but it made the early Christian movement ever more determined:

by the same token that persecution did not smother the hopes of the followers of the 'undesirable' Nazarene, so also the industrial and political tyrants of the twentieth century fail to move the workers from their ideal, which is the emancipation of humanity and the establishment of real civilization.[29]

Although Bellah denies that the tradition of civil religion in America, as he traces it through public addresses of Presidents, was "sectarian" or "in any specific sense Christian,"[30] it is difficult to ignore the Christian qualities it possesses. In the Gettysburg Address, for example, Bellah admits that the Christian theme of "death, sacrifice, and rebirth enters the civil religion,"[31] and Will Herberg, equating American civil religion with a kind of Protestant civic piety, asserts that "American civil religion is compounded of the two great religious movements that molded America—the Puritan Way, secularized; and the Revivalist Way, secularized."[32]

The Jesus depicted in Wobbly journalism has none of the "plainness" and unassuming humbleness which Cuddihy attributes to American Protestant taste and, in turn, American civil religion. He stands heroically against the profit system and, eventually, is hung on a cross—as Carl Sandburg puts it in one of his "Chicago Poems"—at the behest of a "crowd of bankers and business men and lawyers."[33] It is this very class of profiteers, the Wobblies argue, that currently speak the loudest for patriotism and Christian piety. One of America's most vocal clerical proponents of these virtues—and one who suffered perhaps the most vituperous criticism by Wobbly writers—was the popular evangelist, Billy Sunday.

Sunday, a "flamboyant ex–ball player"[34] turned Dwight-Moody-like preacher, took urban America by storm at the turn of the century with "a new combination of old doctrines and up-to-date methods."[35] In his method of preaching, Sunday "utilized almost to perfection the techniques of big business in organizing his campaigns and very large sums of money were subscribed to carry them forward."[36] Unlike the progressive Social Gospel ministers like Rauschenbusch, Gladden and Herron, Billy Sunday and other conservative advocates of "private Protestantism" tended to appeal to America's middle class by essentially accepting the existing social order.[37] Thus, the I.W.W. saw Sunday as antithetical to the rebellious spirit of Jesus because he, like the Salvation Army, urged working people to accept things the way they were, concentrate on personal salvation, and patiently await the "pie-in-the-sky" after death.

In writing about Billy Sunday's "homesickness for Spokane," the editor of the *IW* speculates that the evangelist misses the sound of water bubbling over the falls because it "no doubt reminds him . . . of the tinkle of the coins of the faithful as they drop [them] into the collection boxes at the tabernacle." In a similar tone, the writer continues: "The people who followed Christ for loaves were not up to the standard of Sunday. How much better to follow Christ to some purpose—for thousands of dollars, for instance." In commenting further upon the relationship between Billy Sunday and Jesus, whom the famous evangelist professed to follow, the writer eschews any genuine connection:

We wonder if "Billy" would have been among the disciples of Jesus when Jesus raided the cornfield, by direct action, when he was hungry? Not he! He would have been among the respectable of the time.

Did Billy ever have a word of condemnation for the rich thieves who paid him? Or a good word for the wretches whom they robbed?

But then Sunday has studied the lives of the saints! He must have taken a post-graduate course in the life of Judas Iscariot and Ananias.[38]

Billy Sunday then, in the context of the Wobbly analysis, casts his lot with the ruling class; with the treachery of Judas rather than the rebellion of Jesus. The gospel preached by Sunday was welcomed by employers, the Wobblies said, because it urged workers to submit passively to the present economic system. It is no wonder, says a Wobbly writer in a 1910 article entitled "Superstition," that when Sunday and his "bunch of grafters" came to Bellingham and Everett, Washington, "some of the sawmill companies allowed their slaves to attend the services at the tabernacle on the company's time." In one such service which the writer describes,

Hundreds of workingmen in Everett paraded the street to the tabernacle carrying circular saws with such inscriptions on them as "Employees of Christ." Many of these poor deluded men were working for Weyerhauser (the richest man in the world)[39] for the miserable pittance of $2 and $2.25 a day, and in many instances the wages are as low as $1.75. They looked as if they needed the price of a haircut or a square meal instead of having the HOLY GHOST rammed into them. . . . Billy Sunday did very well in Bellingham and Everett.[40]

Billy Sunday, in many ways, represented a reactionary backlash against the progressive forces of the Social Gospel movement.[41] Politically, the I.W.W.'s opposition to Sunday was in line with all or most of the organizations for social change at the time. Poet Carl Sandburg, for example, in writing to his publisher, Alfred Harcourt, argues, in 1916, for the inclusion of his anti–Billy Sunday poem, "To a Contemporary Bunkshooter," in his *Chicago Poems* collection on the grounds that Sunday is the most conspicuous single embodiment in this country of the crowd leader or crowd operative who uses jungle methods, stark voodoo stage effects, to play hell with democracy. This is the main cause of the fundamental hatred which men have for Sunday.[42]

Although not a member of the I.W.W., Sandburg considered himself a sympathizer, celebrating Bill Haywood in 1907 as "presidential timber, a Whitmanic type" and referring to himself as an I.W.W. without a red card.[43] Furthermore, Sandburg's poem as well as his letter to his publisher seem to mirror the prophetic nature of the I.W.W.'s critique of Sunday. Like the Wobblies, Sandburg saw Billy Sunday as antithetical to Jesus, telling Harcourt:

The only other American figure that might compare with Sunday is Hearst. Both dabble in treacheries of the primitive, invoke terrors of the unknown, utilize sex as a stage prop, and work on elemental fears of the mob, with Hearst the same antithesis to Tom Jefferson that Bill Sunday is to Jesus of Nazareth.[44]

In the poem, the antithesis is made even more dramatic, possessing "the religious strain that should run through real poetry."[45] Addressing himself directly to Sunday, the "contemporary bunkshooter," Sandburg asks bluntly, "what do you know about Jesus?" Despite all his hysterical shirt-tearing and "yelling about Jesus," writes Sandburg, Billy Sunday is actually in league with and having his way paid by "the same crooks and strong-arm men" who "nailed Christ to the cross."[46]

The I.W.W. press, very much like the Sandburg poem, frequently presents the image of Jesus in stark contrast to contemporary "bunkshooters" or "skypilots" who, while professing to speak for Christ, are really doing the bidding of the ruling class or Judas. General Booth and his Salvation Army, for example, often generate a Wobbly scorn comparable to that directed at Billy Sunday.

In an article entitled "In the Holy Name of Cash," I.W.W. writer Jim Seymour attacks a cartoon that appeared in the Chicago *Evening World* (originally called the *Daily Socialist*). After addressing the hypocrisy of the cartoon, intended to celebrate Booth's supposed kindness to the poor, Seymour writes:

in the name of Christ this saintly rascal committed his crimes against the very people of whom Christ is said to have been crucified, yet the artist praises the perfidious sneak who does the very things which Christ condemned. . . . Has he heard that Christ made profits from the renting of lousy bunks? Or didn't he know that Christ himself had no place to lay his head?[47]

Before moving to a second religious area that the I.W.W. press treats—the contradiction between the modern Christian tendency toward preaching peace and the actual practice of supporting war—there is one further religious institution of the period with which the Wobbly press contrasts the figure of the rebel Jesus. The Young Men's Christian Association (Y.M.C.A.), which grew out of the pre–Civil War revival movement of 1857–58,[48] followed the path of the Salvation Army in choosing service to the urban poor as the most effective means of carrying out its evangelical mission.[49] In the period between 1908–09, national staff members E. C. Carter and W. D. Weatherford were instrumental in promoting the national Y.M.C.A. policy of social service to workers and immigrants.[50] Such activities, the I.W.W. argued, served the existing ruling class by appeasing the disinherited while defending the "civil religion" of capitalist America. An example of this interpretation appears in a 1909 *IW* article on a Sunday afternoon meeting of (as the writer refers to it) the "Young Men's Christian Assassination," led by Lieutenant Titus, "the first soldier who scaled the walls of Pekin." The writer continues:

Blessed are the peacemakers, said Christ. Blessed are the warriors and invaders says the Y.M.C.A. Christ, the carpenter's son, would have been kicked down the steps of the Spokane Y.M.C.A. as an agitator and a mere workman. Hypocrisy! Thy mantle is broad! . . . 'Young Men's Christian Association!' Good Lord deliver us. 'Peace on earth.' Imagine Jesus Christ leading a band of marauders, scaling the walls of Pekin! In what way is the morality of the Y.M.C.A. any better than that of the priests of Baal—except the former have less excuse and ought to know better.[51]

This attack on the Y.M.C.A. is the foreshadowing of a Wobbly anti-militarism which reaches a peak as America moves closer to war in Europe. Organized religion, the I.W.W. charged, was guilty of complicity with U.S. capitalism in whipping up American sentiment in favor of this war. Robert T. Handy, in his *A Christian America: Protestant Hopes and Historical Realities*, assesses quite clearly the role of American churches in World War I:

The Protestant hope for world conquest for Christ and civilization was to be realized primarily by voluntary means, by the Spirit, commitment, and sacrifice of those who believed it would soon be realized, with God's help. But when civilization was threatened, then the Protestant forces could include war in their crusading pattern—it happened in 1898, and in a much larger scale it happened in 1917–1918.[52]

Since much has already been written about the I.W.W.'s opposition to World War I and any nationalistic war,[53] little need be said here. The primary concern of this work is the religious dimension of this opposition—specifically, the contradiction which the I.W.W. press reveals between Christian values and militaristic practice. This contradiction, as well as others, was summed up nicely in 1910 by a Minneapolis Wobbly named J. E. Nash. The last stanza of a seven-stanza poem entitled "Theory versus Experience" charges:

> We claim to worship the Prince of Peace,
>   But trust in the sword and gun;
> We pay men pensions for wholesale murder,
>   But hang them for killing one.
> So we conclude its a crime to kill
>   One brother or steal a cent;
> But kill a half a million or steal a full billion
>   YOU'RE BOSS OF THE GOVERNMENT.[54]

Six years later, as America moved toward the brink of the European War, the I.W.W. passed a resolution at its tenth convention, spelling out, in uncompromising terms, the union's firm opposition to militarism:

With the European war for conquest and exploitation raging and destroying our lives, class consciousness and unity of the workers, and the evergrowing agitation for military preparedness clouding the main issues and delaying the realization of our ultimate aim [of the realization of Industrial Democracy] with patriotic and therefore capitalistic aspirations, we openly declare ourselves the determined opponents of all nationalistic sectionalism, or patriotism, and the militarism preached and supported by our enemy, the capitalist class.[55]

In its opposition to militarism and patriotism, the I.W.W. strikes at the very root of American civil religion. For, as Herbert Richardson points out in his essay, "Civil Religion in Theological Perspective," the "basic cultic rite of civil religion is human sacrifice in warfare."[56] In an early article entitled "The Sacrament of War," a Wobbly writer discusses ironically how things have changed from the days when Elijah "is said to have killed the priests of Baal who performed human sacrifices with their own hands." Nowadays, the writer continues,

the priests of Moloch no longer sacrifice babies to the image of their gods. How much nobler to sacrifice our brothers and sons and husbands to the god of dollars! And the priests, what of them? They are upholding the justice of the legalized murder; they are still possessing the minds of the children with false ideas of patriotism. But the sublime thing about the sky-pilots is the matchless hypocrisy.[57]

This hypocrisy which the Wobbly writer quoted above condemned in 1909, intensified greatly in 1916–17, illustrating, as Handy points out, that "the Protestant forces could include war in their crusading pattern." In condemning the "reptilious press" and preachers who sought to make the European war appear as a Christian crusade, the editor of the *IW* writes in 1917,

We don't believe it. If he is a God of peace, love and brotherhood and he is anywhere on earth, it must be in China or the other heathen nations. Even the devil, bad as his reputation is, would not be guilty of the crimes with which they are trying to saddle God. No God or devil would ever fall so low as to fight for the American munition trusts.[58]

To the Wobblies, American capitalism was conducting a two-front war: against the European working class abroad and against the American working class at home. Both wars, they argue, demonstrate the hollowness of patriotism and American civil religion. In a voice echoing the rage of the Biblical prophets condemning the decadent order, the editor of the *IW* cried out in the summer of 1916:

How long will murder crazed plutocracies and social pirates lay the skeletons of their murdered victims at the feet of civilization? How long will they lay the corpses of thousands, millions of workers, in the name of Christ, on the altars of a Christ who said, 'Blessed are the peacemakers'?[59]

Those who oppose such slaughter, says another editorial a year later, are brutally suppressed. In discussing the fate of all rebels who preach the "propaganda of love," whether in the factories of America or on the fields of Europe, the editor asserts that the

propaganda of love is not new in the history of mankind. There is an old, old book dedicated in part to this propaganda, which we would quote more oftener were it not that we do not want the *IW* suppressed. This propaganda has been tried for twenty centuries and despite some efforts to make it a success, every nation, every corporation in the world is a monument to its failure.

Crucified in the first centuries, all who truly stand for this gospel are equally crucified today.[60]

The parallel is obvious, and appears often in the Wobbly press: the I.W.W., like Jesus, is despised and persecuted because it preaches the gospel of love and solidarity, of human dignity as superior to the profit system. The working class, says one Wobbly writer in recalling the Everett case in which seventy-four free-speech fighters went on trial in Washington,[61] "is also despised and rejected, as was the carpenter of Galilee; yes, and even crucified as he was! Nailed upon the cross of profit to satisfy the blood-lust of the employers of industry."[62]

Such a parallel between the suffering of Jesus and persecution of labor radicals—or between the I.W.W. and religion generally—illustrates the final area for discussion of the I.W.W. press. Wobbly editor Covington Hall, whose Blake-like revolutionary poetry will be examined in the following chapter, makes a provocative philosophical observation in an *IW* article entitled "Where No Vision Is, The People Perish." While declaring that the working class and the employing class have nothing in common—"their law is not our law, their morals are not our morals, their Gods are not our Gods"—he nevertheless insists that,

All revolutions have and must center around some great ideal, some sublime, heart-stirring conception of the "world as it ought to be," and that the American working class will not accomplish anything so long as it cannot dream higher than the Socialist party's ideal of "ten dollars a day for four hours a day."

Framing his call for a controlling vision in more religious terms, Hall speaks of the Wobbly ideal contained in the motto "An Injury to one is an injury to all," declaring that with such an ideal " . . . God has never quarreled, but the priesthoods and the ministeries have ever jeered its champions on their way to Calvary."[63]

This "vision," in order to be acceptably "religious" in Wobbly terms, must be tempered by struggle and sacrifice on behalf of the working class. In a Western Federation of Miners pitch for mine workers to join the union, for example (quoted in the *IW*), the writer asserts that all social change or new doctrines have been brought about by "some man or body of men who have been unsatisfied to continue in the same narrow path." Continuing this popular argument, the writer says: "Of such characters were the first Christians, and such was the character of those who suffered torture and death that the doctrine of Christianity might be established."[64] Similarly, if being religious means "finding out what is right and then doing it," says a Wobbly letter writer who calls himself "Abe R. Deen," then the I.W.W., especially the free-speech fighters who have gone to jail for their beliefs, are "all religious."[65]

In viewing "religion" as a controlling vision of solidarity combined with heroic struggle against the ruling class, the

Wobblies occasionally end up describing their union as a religion. This comparison proved particularly useful in the I.W.W.'s efforts to defend themselves against attacks by business interests in the Western free-speech fights. Protesting that the arrest of free-speech fighters was a violation of the right to freedom of religion, one I.W.W. wrote, in a "Call to Action":

The Constitution says that "Congress shall make no law respecting an establishment, or prohibiting the free exercise thereof. . . . Industrial Unionism is our religion, as through it we will have peace on earth. It is denied us in Spokane."[66]

The I.W.W.'s attitude toward Christianity, then, as revealed in its press, is too complex to dismiss simply as unbridled hostility. Rather than tossing Christianity on the ash-heap of history, the I.W.W. declares, in the words of Walker P. Smith, that "the working class and the employing class have no God in common," and if the workers feel the need for a God, it should be one "of the working class, by the working class, for the working class." (*IW*, 7/2/10, p. 3) Within this context, the Industrial Workers of the World rejects bourgeois "civil religion" as idolatry and Billy Sunday revivalism as hypocrisy, while celebrating the heroism of Jesus who, like martyr Joe Hill, lived like a rebel and died like a rebel.

NOTES

1. Joseph R. Conlin, ed., *The American Radical Press: 1880–1960*, V. 1 (Westport, Connecticut: Greenwood Press, 1974), p. 131.

2. Philip S. Foner, *The Industrial Workers of the World: 1905–1917* (New York: International Publishers, 1965), p. 148.

3. Henry F. May, *The End of American Innocence: A Study of the First Years of Our Own Time* (New York: Alfred A. Knopf, 1959), p. 178.

4. Quoted by Melvyn Dubofsky in *We Shall Be All* (New York: Quadrangle Press, 1969), p. 350.

5. *IW*, August 26, 1909, p. 4.

6. *IW*, March 18, 1909, p. 1.

7. *IW*, July 1, 1909, p. 2.

8. *IW*, June 17, 1916, p. 3.

9. *IW*, September 10, 1910, p. 3.

10. *IW*, February 3, 1917, p. 3.

11. Dubofsky, *We Shall Be All*, p. 154.

12. E. J. Hobsbawm, *Primitive Rebels: Studies in Archaic Forms of Social Movement in the 19th and 20th Century* (Manchester, England: Manchester University Press, 1959), p. 57.

13. Dubofsky, p. 154.

14. Hobsbawm, p. 57.

15. Ibid., p. 59.

16. Paul Tillich, *Political Expectation* (New York: Harper and Row Publishers, 1971), p. 150.

17. Ibid.

18. Roland Robertson, *The Sociological Interpretation of Religion* (New York: Schocken Books, 1970), p. 166.

19. *Industrial Union Bulletin*, May 16, 1908, p. 1.

20. Robert T. Handy, *A Christian America: Protestant Hopes and Historical Realities* (London: Oxford University Press, 1971), pp. 163–164.

21. Quotes from a poem, "The Proletariare," by Stanislaus Cullen, published on July 23, 1910, issue of the *IW* (p. 2).

22. "The Civil Religion Debate," Russell E. Richey and Donald G. Jones, eds. *American Civil Religion* (New York: Harper and Row, 1974), p. 3.

23. Robert N. Bellah, "Civil Religion in America," Ibid., p. 21.

24. Introduction, Ibid., p. 16.

25. Martin E. Marty, "Two Kinds of Civil Religion" (p. 141) and Herbert Richardson "Civil Religion in Theological Perspective" (p. 169) from *American Civil Religion*.

26. The expression Sidney E. Mead borrows from G. K. Chesterton to present his concept of civil religion as a "religion of the republic."

27. John F. Kendrick, "Christians at War," *Songs of the Workers: To Fan the Flames of Discontent*, 34th edition (Chicago: I.W.W., 1973), p. 12. First appeared in the 9th edition, 1913.

28. John Murray Cuddihy, *No Offense: Civil Religion and Protestant Taste* (New York: Seabury Press, 1978).

29. *IUB*, January 11, 1908, p. 3.

30. Bellah, "Civil Religion in America," p. 29.

31. Ibid., p. 31.

32. Will Herberg, "America's Civil Religion: What It Is and Whence It Comes," *American Civil Religion*, p. 83.

33. Carl Sandburg, "To a Contemporary Bunkshooter," *Chicago Poems* (Henry Holt and Co., 1916). Included in *Complete Poems* (New York: Harcourt, Brace and World, 1950).

34. Martin E. Marty, *Righteous Empire: The Protestant Experience in America* (New York: Dial Press, 1970), p. 183.

35. May, *The End of American Innocence*, p. 126.

36. William Warren Sweet, *Revivalism in America* (New York: Abingdon Press, 1944), p. 170.

37. Marty, *Righteous Empire*, p. 187.

38. *IW*, March 18, 1909, p. 2. Ananais was a man in the Bible who was struck dead for lying about his having stolen the church's money (Acts 5: 1–5).

39. John Philip Weyerhauser (1858–1935) was the son of the German-born "Lumber King," Frederick. John was a successful lumber and timber magnate, president of Weyerhauser Timber Co., who settled in Tacoma, Washington.

40. "Superstition," *IW*, December 1, 1910, p. 2.

41. Marty, *Righteous Empire*, p. 211.

42. *The Letters of Carl Sandburg*, ed. Herbert Mitgang (New York: Harcourt, Brace and World, 1968), pp. 108–109.

43. Sandburg, *Letters*. The reference to Haywood appears in an August 19, 1908, letter to Reuben W. Burough (p. 50) and his remark that "I am an I.W.W. but I don't carry a red card" was made in an October, 1919, letter to Romain Roland (p. 169).

44. Ibid., p. 109.

45. Ibid., p. 108.

46. Sandburg, "To a Contemporary Bunkshooter," *Complete Poems*, p. 29.

47. *IW*, September 12, 1912, p. 4.

48. Sandra S. Sizer, *Gospel Hymns and Social Religion: The Rhetoric of Nineteenth-Century Revivalism* (Philadelphia: Temple University Press, 1978) and Marty, *Righteous Empire*, p. 99.

49. Marty, *Righteous Empire*, p. 163.

50. Charles Howard Hopkins, *The Rise of the Social Gospel in American Protestantism, 1865–1915* (New Haven: Yale University Press, 1940), p. 299.

51. *IW*, May 13, 1909, p. 2.

52. Robert T. Handy, *A Christian America: Protestant Hopes and Historical Realities* (London: Oxford University Press, 1971), p. 151.

53. Most of the I.W.W. studies previously mentioned treat the issue of the I.W.W. and World War I. One of the best analyses is Chapter 14 of Dubofsky's *We Shall Be All*, entitled "The Class War at Home and Abroad, 1914–1917," pp. 349–375.

54. *IW*, February 19, 1910, p. 3.

55. Minutes of the 10th Convention of the I.W.W., 1916, p. 138.

Entire resolution is quoted by Fred W. Thompson and Patrick Murfin in *The I.W.W.: Its First Seventy Years* (Chicago: I.W.W., 1976), pp. 109–110.

56. Essay included in *American Civil Religion*, Richey and Jones, p. 174.

57. *IW*, June 3, 1909, p. 2.

58. Editorial entitled "So They Say, But——", *IW*, February 17, 1917, p. 2.

59. *IW*, July 1, 1916, p. 3.

60. *IW*, September 22, 1917, p. 2.

61. See Chapter 23, "The Everett Massacre," in Foner's book.

62. *IW*, March 3, 1917, p. 7.

63. *IW*, August 26, 1909, p. 4.

64. *IW*, June 24, 1909, p. 3.

65. *IW*, January 4, 1912, p. 3.

66. *IW*, February 26, 1910, p. 2.

5

The Poetics of Revolutionary Unionism

Carl Sandburg, in writing to his editor about his Billy Sunday poem, "To a Contemporary Bunkshooter," speaks of "the religious strain that should run through all real poetry."[1] Wobbly songwriter, poet, and editor, Ralph Chaplin, discovered this strain in the poetry of Walt Whitman. After reading *Leaves of Grass*, a work that radical publisher "Comrade" Charles H. Kerr had recommended as "rebel poetry of the highest order," Chaplin experienced a metaphysical revelation of such force that, from that moment on, "Karl Marx and Kropotkin had very keen competition."[2] Such expostulations on the spiritual force of poetry might seem strange coming from two such articulate proponents of "the people" as Sandburg and Chaplin. If one reads closely the poetry that often appears in the I.W.W. press, however, it is difficult to miss the religious spirit that appears congruently with the radical messages of industrial unionism and agitation for the overthrow of capitalism.

Although Wobbly writers usually found the medium of music much more conducive to the winning of worker recruits, the pages of the I.W.W. newspapers and other publications abound in poetry. Granted, these works are often not of conspicuous literary merit; nevertheless, they frequently possess a wit and poetic strength that attracted the radicalizing workers who read the Wobbly press. Furthermore, they frequently reveal a great deal about the religious texture of the I.W.W. message, particularly the sectarian quality and prophetic "voice" of that mes-

sage. All five of the Wobbly poets that will be examined here—
Joe Hill, Arturo Giovannitti, Charles Ashleigh, Ralph Chaplin, and Covington Hall—use the vehicle of poetry to advocate
a revolutionary solution to the social problems of the time. As
artists and I.W.W. radicals, these five poets often resemble most
alienated intellectuals of the Progressive Era who attacked the
existing economic and cultural paradigms. As Amos N. Wilder
says in his discussion of modern poetry in *The Spiritual Aspects of the New Poetry*,

Where men of our time . . . achieve a sufficient stability of person-
ality and are alienated from the orthodox religious traditions, their
religious quest often takes the form of social revolution in some form.[3]

Such was certainly the case with the five Wobbly poets to
be discussed here. Before examining the lives and works of the
poets themselves, it is necessary to comment briefly on the
genre of poetry as a vehicle for proletarian thought, particularly as reflected in Wobbly verse. The I.W.W. poets, like most
revolutionaries, rejected soundly the art-for-art's-sake function of poetry which flourished in the nineteenth century and
which "proposed itself really as a form of, or substitute for, religion."[4] The Wobbly poets wished to separate themselves as
far as possible from this tradition. Ralph Chaplin, for example, as quoted by Scott Nearing in his introduction to Chaplin's book of prison poems, *Bars and Shadows*, declares une-
quivocally:

Above all things, I don't want anyone to try to make me out a 'poet'—
because I'm not. I don't think much of these esthetic creatures who
condescend to stoop to our level that we may have the blessings of
culture. We'll manage to make our own—do it in our own way, and
stagger through somehow . . . these are tremendous times, and sooner
or later someone will come along big enough to sound the right note,
and it will be a rebel note.[5]

In removing himself from the realm of those "esthetic creatures" who celebrate art for art's sake and who substitute poetry for religion, Ralph Chaplin—like the other four poets—
took on another role: the poet as prophetic rebel. Many young

poets between the years 1912–1917—a period that might be seen as the "rebellion" in American poetry[6]—saw themselves as social rebels. In fulfilling this role, the artists of the pre–World War I period, unlike the propagandists for "socialist realism" of a later period, believed they could win people to the revolution through the zeal of their "spontaneity and self-expression"[7] rather than through the formulaic adherence to a "party line" or "correct social dogma." Genevieve Taggard, in her introduction to an anthology of verse from the *Masses* and the *Liberator* (which includes poems by Giovannitti, Ashleigh and Chaplin), summarizes the attitude toward their craft held by the pre–World War I rebel poets:

> The artist's concern is not to persuade or educate, but to overpoweringly express. A good revolutionist should allow the artist this freedom, since he knows very well that only liberals seek to persuade, or to lure other half-hearted liberals into action.
> The working class needs artists. It has no one to convince of its quality but itself.[8]

Joe Hill, born Joseph Emmanuel Haaglund, was certainly a working class artist in addition to being "the I.W.W.'s most famous folk poet and martyr."[9] Born in Sweden, Hill emigrated to the United States with his brother in 1902, writing songs and poems as he traveled westward, supporting himself with a variety of jobs ranging from stacking wheat to digging copper.[10] As Wobblies Fred Thompson and Dean Nolan point out in *Joe Hill: I.W.W. Songwriter*, "few hard facts are known about Joe Hill's first ten years in America. Although there are a number of stories about the places he had been and the things that he had done . . . few can be substantiated."[11] Hill's life does not become "public record," it might be said, until after his arrest on January 13, 1914, on the charge of murdering a Salt Lake City grocer and ex-policeman, J. B. Morrison. After a twenty-two-month legal battle that made the case one of the most well-known defense struggles in labor history, Joe Hill was executed by a Utah firing squad on November 19, 1915.[12]

Much has been written about the tremendously insubstantial, largely circumstantial charges resulting in Hill's death. The concern here is not as much with the case of Joe Hill as it is with Hill's poetry and the poems inspired by his "martyr-hood." Celebrating the influence of Hill's life and death, Joyce Kornbluh writes:

His songs continued to be sung over the world. "The Preacher and the Slave" and "Casey Jones" became American folk songs, and "pie in the sky" a slogan for a generation in the 1930's. Hill, the man, became a legend compared to Paul Bunyan, John Henry, Johnny Appleseed, and other folk heroes—preserved by novelists, playwrights, poets and researchers. His story has inspired more writing than any other labor hero.[13]

Although George Milburn, in *The Hobo's Hornbook*, refers to Hill as the "hobo's poet laureate,"[14] it was primarily the songs rather than the scattered doggerel verse of Joe Hill that made him such a prominent "folk poet" among workers, hoboes, and eventually, the general public. As pointed out in a previous chapter, those songs often parodied organized religion and bourgeois morality. "The harsh, tough, skeptical songs of Joe Hill convey most clearly the nature of the I.W.W.'s appeal to well-brought-up intellectuals of radical sympathies. Here, if anywhere, was a clear breach with timidity, moralism, and the whole manner and content of the standard American culture."[15] His earliest parody, "The Preacher and the Slave," which circulated among workers on song cards before it appeared in the 1911 edition of the I.W.W. songbook,[16] offers an alternative morality to the preacher's "pie-in-the-sky" ethic of "work and pray, live on hay." In contrast to the passive doctrine of quietly waiting for a future salvation, Hill's song offers an activist rebel's creed: "Working men of all countries unite,/Side by side we for freedom will fight."

In fact, an essential value permeating Wobbly poetry is the strong preference for action over passivity or contemplation, militancy over conciliation or "reasonable" discussion. As in the apocalyptic poetry of William Blake—which re-emerges in Covington Hall's *Songs of Love and Rebellion*—Joe Hill saw evil as the negation of action, as "peaceful coexistence" with the ruling class. Revolutionary action, for Joe Hill, might occasionally involve violence for, as Georges Sorel wrote in his influential work, *Reflections on Violence*—a work published in 1905 and found often in Wobbly libraries:[17]

People who have devoted their life to a cause which they identify with the regeneration of the world could not hesitate to make use of any weapon which might serve to develop to a greater degree the spirit of the class war, seeing that greater efforts were being made to suppress it.[18]

A short poem by Hill entitled "Rebel's Toast," published in *Solidarity* five months after his arrest, illustrates the poet's advocacy of sabotage (symbolized by the wooden shoe) when necessary for the advancement of the working class:

> If freedom's road seems rough and hard,
>   And strewn with rocks and thorns,
> Then put your wooden shoe on, pard,
>   And you won't hurt your corns.
> To organize and teach, no doubt,
>   Is very good—that's true,
> But still we can't succeed without
> The Good Ole Wooden Shoe.[19]

The message of direct action and solidarity which permeates Hill's songs and poems, together with the heroic manner in which he faced his impending execution, illustrates why "Hill was a literary martyr of the American proletariat."[20] The martyr image, as Gibbs M. Smith points out in his comprehensive work on Hill, was consciously cultivated by the rebel songwriter himself (in such statements as "I have lived like an artist, I shall die like an artist" and "Don't waste time mourning—Organize!") as well as by the I.W.W.[21] As Wobbly poetry and prose often illustrate, this martyrhood is sometimes paralleled with the crucifixion of Christ. Hill himself pointed out to Elizabeth Gurley Flynn, when she came to visit him in jail, that he was the age "when Jesus was crucified."[22] Similarly, after Hill's execution on November 19, 1915, Mary Latham painted a strikingly colorful twelve-by-twelve foot mural depicting Hill, strapped on a chair, receiving the rifle bullets in his heart as the image of the crucified Jesus emerges from the rifle smoke.[23]

The best Wobbly poetry, writes Alan Calmer in his 1934 *New Masses* article, "dealt with their heroes who were killed in battle."[24] It is in such poetry, as well, that one finds evidence of the religious flavor of a good deal of Wobbly literature. Most importantly, as mentioned earlier, much of this poetry contains a strong element of martyrhood, a force that unifies the membership of many social movements. Sorel's comments on this matter are enlightening:

The Christian ideology was based on these rather rare but very heroic events; there was no necessity for the martyrdoms to be numerous in order to prove, by the test of experience, the absolute truth of the new religion and the absolute error of the old, to establish thus that there were two incompatible ways, and to make clear that the reign of evil would come to an end.[25]

The I.W.W., writes Gibbs M. Smith, "tenderly preserved its martyrs within the pages of the 'Little Red Songbook.' "[26] Besides Hill, these martyrs include Wesley Everest and Frank Little, two Wobblies who were tortured and lynched by mobs. The poem by Ralph Chaplin entitled "Wesley Everest," printed in the *Industrial Pioneer* in July of 1921, draws a dramatic parallel between the martyrhood of a Wobbly hero and that of Jesus Christ. Everest, a Wobbly lumberjack who had served as a soldier in France at a time when the I.W.W. was being accused in federal courts of conspiring to impede the U.S. war effort, was murdered by a lynch mob in Centralia, Washington, in November 1919.[27] Chaplin's poem, frequently reprinted in the Wobbly press, makes the parallel between Everest and Christ unmistakable:

> Torn and defiant as a wind-lashed reed,
> Wounded he faced you as he stood at bay;
> You dared not lynch him in the light of day,
> But on your dungeon stones you let him bleed;
> Night came . . . and you black vigilants of Greed
> Like human wolves, seized hard upon your prey,
> Tortured and killed . . . and silently slunk away

Without one qualm of horror at the deed.
Once . . . long ago . . . do you remember how
You hailed Him king for soldiers to deride—
You placed a scroll above his bleeding brow
And spat upon Him, scourged Him, crucified . . .
A rebel unto Caesar—then as now
Alone, thorn-crowned, a spear wound in his side![28]

Although Chaplin's earlier poem on the execution of Joe Hill does not contain as obvious a Christian allusion as the Everest poem, it does express the related themes of martyrhood and sacrifice. And, like other Wobbly poems, it illustrates the psychological counterpart to these themes: the "psychology of persecution," one of the twenty-one features of a religious sect that Liston Pope enumerates in his influential sociological study of 1942, *Millhands and Preachers*.[29] Although Pope is primarily concerned with religious sectarianism, the qualities of the sect—as discussed by Weber, Troeltsch, Niebuhr and others—apply frequently to the I.W.W., especially when one considers that the chief characteristic Pope attributes to the sect is the element of protest. When protest gives way to reconciliation, Pope believes, the sect begins the inevitable transformation from the "sect type" to the "church type" of organization.[30] If a sect is to remain a sect, if it is to continue to be what Weber calls "a community of personal believers of the reborn,"[31] it must maintain its identity as a protest body.

Chaplin's poem—"Joe Hill: Murdered by the Authorities of the State of Utah, November the 19th, 1915"—exhibits both the sectarian spirit of protest and the psychology of persecution. The latter, which functions to instill a strong group solidarity among the members of the "sect," is a quality evident in much Wobbly poetry. The Chaplin poem, appearing in the ninth edition of the I.W.W. songbook and frequently reprinted, evokes strongly the themes of sacrifice, persecution, rebellion and martyrhood:

High head and back unbending—fearless and true,
Into the night unending; why was it you?

Heart that was quick with song, turn with their lead;
Life that was young and strong, shattered and dead.

Singer of manly songs, laughter and tears;
Singer of Labor's wrongs, joys, hopes and fears.

Though you were one of us, what could we do?
Joe, there were none of us needed like you.

We gave, however small, what Life could give;
We would have given all that you might live.

Your death you held as naught, slander and shame;
We from the very thought shrank as from flame.

Each of us held his breath, tense with despair,
You, who were close to Death, seemed not to care.

White-handed loathsome power, knowing no pause,
Sinking in labor's flower, murderous claws;

Boastful, with leering eyes, blood-dripping jaws . . .
Accurst be the cowardice hidden in laws!

Utah has drained your blood; white hands are wet;
We of the "surging flood" *never forget!*

Our songster! have your laws now had their fill?
Know, ye, his songs and cause ye cannot kill.

High head and back unbending—"rebel true blue,"
Into the night unending; why was it you?[32]

This poem, perhaps the most popular work of its time written in commemoration of Hill's death, is filled with contrasting images of capitalist "law" ("loathsome power," "murderous power," "murderous claws," "cowardice," "boastful," "leering," "blood dripping") and proletarian heroism ("life," "labor's flower," "young," "strong," "high head," "surging flood"). Such contrasts, which permeate the works of Chaplin, illustrate an important element of sectarianism.

The debate over the church-type and sect-type classifications has occupied the sociology of religion for the past several decades.[33] One could avoid being embroiled in this controversy, however, by asserting that, "a church is a religious group that accepts the social environment in which it exists," while, "a sect is a religious group that rejects the social environment in which it exists."[34] Sect formation is generally "an expression of alienation, it is a movement of people who are spiritually, socially, economically, educationally or in other ways 'disinherited.' "[35] Simply put, one could describe the church or denomination as culturally dominant and the sect as alienated or disinherited.

Two events in 1912 give credence to this dichotomy—both involve radicalism and religion. Eugene V. Debs, who "showed a surprising measure of religious openness," won nearly a million votes in the Presidential election of 1912, an election in which the loosely formed Christian Socialist Federation teamed up with the Socialist Party to help bring about this impressive result. Eight years earlier, George D. Herron, the Minneapolis Congregational minister, had given the nominating speech for Debs at the Socialist Party's 1904 Chicago convention.[36] As Dubofsky writes, "Debs was American-born and, though a professed non-believer, a Christian almost by instinct. Debs Americanized and Christianized the socialist movement." He continues:

By doing so he made it acceptable, respectable, almost popular. For many followers who still retained traditional religious beliefs, Debs portrayed the essence of the Christ figure: the simple, humble carpenter who sacrifices himself to redeem a corrupt society.[37]

When one considers the broad support Debs was able to gain among "progressive" Christians, it is not so surprising that he was able to amass such a hefty vote count in 1912.

Another major event of 1912 was the famous Lawrence, Massachusetts textile strike, the most important labor victory for the I.W.W. The strike, written about in great detail by virtually every historian of the I.W.W., gained tremendous support from all quarters of society. Even the "dean" of American letters, William Dean Howells, wrote an article deploring the police violence during the notorious "children's crusade," an exodus of workers' children from the "class war" situation in Lawrence which was met by brutal police intervention.[38] Although the events of the strike itself are well known,[39] a feature less often discussed is the sectarian nature of the I.W.W.'s participation in the later months of the strike as well as an important Wobbly poet who emerged from the struggle at Lawrence. An essential element of a sect, as discussed by Liston Pope in his *Millhands and Preachers*, is protest.

In contrast to the "popular" radicalism of Debs, the Wobblies maintained unflinchingly a class struggle perspective throughout the strike. While this stance gained massive support during the early winter months of the strike, resulting in a major labor victory by the end of March,[40] the middle-class Progressive publication, *Survey*, was to ask in April:

Are we to expect that instead of playing the game respectably . . . the laborers are to listen to . . . such strange doctrines as these of "direct action," "sabotage," "syndicalism," "the general strike," and "violence"?

If Lawrence workers are to fall prey to the propaganda of the Wobblies instead of "playing the game respectable," the article warns, then the "current morality" and the "sacredness of property and even life itself" is under attack.[41]

When religion played a role in the Lawrence strike, it was not in the spirit of the reconciliation and harmony of the Debs campaign, but in the sectarian spirit of alienation, of the disinherited against the dominant social environment. This spirit is captured in Joe Hill's song, "John Golden and the Lawrence Strike." Written to the tune of "A Little Talk with Jesus," Hill aims his satirical arrow at the collaboration between John Golden, conservative head of the A.F.L.'s United Textile Workers, and mill owner William Wood. This song, written while Hill was in San Diego participating in the free-speech fight there,[42] is one of the most devastating attacks on "business unionism" ever written. The second stanza illustrates nicely the alienation that the Wobbly "folk poets" frequently expressed toward the controlling social institutions of the middle class:

> The preachers, cops and money kings were walking hand in
> hand,
> The boys in blue, with stars and stripes, were sent by Uncle
> Sam;
> Still things were looking blue, cause every striker knew
> That weaving cloth with bayonetts is hard to do.[43]

But realizing that the majority of workers in Lawrence and in Boston joined with the Citizen's Association in denouncing the leadership of the strike,[44] the Wobblies played down their opposition to the "skypilots" that opposed them. For the most part, the I.W.W. followed what Elizabeth Gurley Flynn declared "a correct labor policy during the strike" which meant "we did not discuss religion and warned all speakers, regardless of their personal views, not to offend the religious feelings of the people."[45] Nevertheless, on September 30 an event occurred that offered ammunition to the anti-Wobbly forces that sought to equate the I.W.W. with atheism.

In protest against the arrest and fabricated murder charge against two important strike leaders, Joseph Ettor and Arturo Giovannitti, several thousand Italian anarchists marched through the streets of Lawrence, several of them carrying a prominent banner which read "No God! No Master!"[46] This iconoclastic gesture, although disclaimed by the Wobbly press (Flynn even said the "banner was worth a million dollars to the employers and may have been a deliberate act of provocation"[47]), seriously undercut the Wobblies' organizing efforts in Lawrence after the strike victory in March. As surely as Debs' friendly overtures to the Christian Socialist Federation won him the warm approval of "progressive" Christians, the September 30 event served to inflate the hostility of many Christians toward the I.W.W.

Although the Wobblies neither instigated nor approved of this event, its response to it illustrated, in Flynn's words, the I.W.W.'s "lack of any central authority to control situations."[48] It also illustrated, one might argue, the difficult time the I.W.W. had distancing itself from a slogan that, while not Wobbly inspired, seemed to reflect the I.W.W.'s alienation from the dominant social institutions. Also, this event, provoking a giant sweep of anti-labor, anti-Wobbly sentiment, marked the termination of any major influence the I.W.W. had in Lawrence.[49]

Out of the Lawrence struggle, however, emerged one of the I.W.W.'s most articulate poetic voices. Arturo Giovannitti, who was eventually cleared, with Joseph Ettor, of the false charges of inciting violence and being an accessory to murder, began the literary phase of his radical career as editor of the Italian socialist newspaper, *Il Proletario*.[50] He was, as Wobbly Charles Ashleigh writes, "a remarkable man of remarkable antecedents" who "emigrated from his native Italy at the age of seventeen, and was precipitated into our whirl of economic struggles."[51] More specifically, Justus Ebert, director of publicity for the I.W.W. during the Giovannitti-Ettor case, says in an *IW* article that Giovannitti was born of upper-middle-class parents in 1884 in Campobasso, Abruzzi, Italy, but emigrated to America in the year 1900.[52]

In discussing Giovannitti's well-known poem, "The Cage," a writer for the "Contributor's Club" in the *Atlantic Monthly* offers this interesting piece of biographical material on the poet:

After encountering many varied experiences of an immigrant in search of a livelihood, he entered the Union Theological Seminary in New York with the purpose of becoming a minister of the Presbyterian church. Although he never graduated, Giovannitti saw actual service in conducting Presbyterian missions in more than one city, and interested himself in the work of the church, until Socialism came to impersonate religion in his life and led him through the vanishing stages of unbelief into atheism. During the Lawrence strike Giovannitti preached with missionary intensity the doctrine of Syndicalism.[53]

What this writer for the decidedly non-syndicalist *Atlantic* fails to recognize is that Giovannitti, as he passed through "the vanishing stages of unbelief into atheism," retained a good deal of the Christian ideas he no doubt acquired at Union Theological Seminary. The poem "The Cage," printed in the same issue of the *Atlantic* in which the review appears, provides a dramatic example of the religious quality of Giovannitti's poetry.

The critic in the *Atlantic* review, while asserting that "if there is a poetry of anarchy, this is it," recognizes also the spiritual quality of the work. "We are not prepared to debate the question whether syndicalism has a soul," writes the reviewer, "but if it has, 'The Cage' gives a picture of it." Although admitting that "the philosophy of the poem sounds harshly materialistic," the reviewer reminds the readers that "to the very poor,

bread, bed, and sunshine may suggest something very different from materialism. They are helps—almost essential helps—
to spiritual freedom."[54]

The famed Helen Keller, who wrote the introduction to
Giovannitti's 1914 collection of poems, *Arrow in the Gale*, approaches the poetry from a critical perspective quite different
from the *Atlantic* reviewer's. As a socialist and a materialist
herself, she does not feel an obligation to justify the materialism of Giovannitti's poetry on the grounds that material
goods—in satisfying the basic human needs—lead to "spiritual freedom." Rather, to the charge that Giovannitti's poetry
is "rashly materialistic," she asserts:

So is Homer. So is Virgil. So is Dante. So is Shakespeare. So is Shelley. So are allegories and parables. So are the prophecies of Isaiah.
So is the description of the New Jerusalem descending out of Heaven,
at once most spirit-illumined and most closely linked with the natural needs, the sensuous pleasure and desires of man.

For Giovannitti, as for many of the writers in the Wobbly
press, the value of the "belly need" is inextricably connected
with the less material needs of the workers. Like Shelley, "a
poet of revolt against the cruelty, the poverty, which too many
of us accept in blind content," writes Keller, Giovannitti provides the reader with a poetry that is "the spiritualization of
a lofty dream that he seeks to realize—the establishment of
love and brotherhood and social justice for every man and
woman upon earth."[55]

This lofty dream is embodied powerfully in "The Cage." It,
like "The Walker" and "The Praise of Spring," often won critical acclaim for being "unsurpassed in power by anything ever
published in America."[56] This poem—in which Giovannitti
"deals with the mummy of authority"[57]—evokes dramatically
the spirit of the sect. Unlike the "large number of prosperous
and popular religious organizations" that flourish in the United
States, the sect, as suggested earlier, is a voluntary fellowship
of converts which forms "a community apart from and in opposition to the world around it."[58] Like much of the New Left
rhetoric of the 1960's, the sect often presents its argument in

an us-vs.-them dichotomy. For the New Left, this clash was seen as existing between the Youth (or Life) Culture and the Death Culture of the Establishment,[59] between the New World ready to be born, and the Old World preparing to meet its death.

In "The Cage," Giovannitti draws the lines very distinctly between the dying world of the old and the vital world of the new—the "new society" struggling to be born within "the shell of the old." The poem was written in Salem, Massachusetts, where Giovannitti was incarcerated—with Joseph Ettor and Joseph Caruso—following their January 29 arrest in Lawrence. The occasion for the arrest was a protest parade which resulted in gunfire between strikers and police and in the death of a bystander, Anna Lo Pizzo. Despite the strikers' claims that policeman Oscar Benoit had fired the fatal shot, Joseph Caruso was arrested for the murder and, although they were not present at the parade, Ettor and Giovannitti were arrested for inciting the riot.[60] In the opening lines of the poem, Giovannitti paints a striking picture of the hoary appearance of their captors:

> In the middle of the great greenish room stood the green iron cage.
> All was old, and cold and mournful, ancient with the double antiquity of heart and brain in the great greenish room.
> Old and hoary was the man who sat upon the faldstool, upon the fireless and godless altar. . . .
> Senility, dullness and dissolution were all around the green iron cage, and nothing was new and young and alive in the great room, except the three men who were in the cage.[61]

"The contrast is drawn," writes Charles Ashleigh, "between the outworn formalities and rites of the law and the lusty life of labor,—between the dead lives of the dismal practitioners of a stilted and tyrannical formula and the life of vigorous conflict of the awakening working class."[62] In contrast to the "senility, dullness and dissolution" that surrounds them, "all the sweetness of all the wholesome odors of the world outside was redolent in the breath of the three men in the cage."

At the end of the poem, the iron of the bars of the cage cries out to the three men—it is the Biblical prophetic voice of justice in the face of oppression:

O Man, remold me with thy wonderful
hands into an instrument of thy toil,
Remake of me the sword of thy justice,
Remake of me the sickle for thy grain.
Remake of me the oven for thy bread,
And the andirons for thy peaceful hearth,
O Man!

The poetry of Giovannitti virtually vibrates with the voice of prophecy, the voice of righteousness crying out in the wilderness against the world "bound in the chains of the past" shackled by "the police, the law, the church, another age shackling this."[63] To use Max Weber's terminology, it is the voice of the "emissary prophet," such as the ancient Hebrew prophets concerned with people joining together in pursuit of justice, rather than the "exemplary prophet" like Buddha whose message is one of personal enlightenment.[64] Although the prophetic voice permeates much of Giovannitti's poetry, it is perhaps never so eloquent as in his famous "Sermon on the Common." This poem/address was delivered during the first days of the Lawrence strike to workers of nearly twenty-five different nationalities—what Elizabeth Gurley Flynn refers to as a "veritable tower of Babel." As Flynn writes, "All the strikers gathered on the Lawrence Common so that the workers could realize their oneness and strength." It was here, she continues, "that Giovannitti delivered his beautiful 'Sermon on the Common.' "[65]

The "sermon" is, in effect, Christ's "Sermon on the Mount" turned on its head, with strength substituted for meekness, rebels for peacemakers, revenge for mercy and, of course, the kingdom of earth for the kingdom of heaven. The opening "beatitudes" capture the flavor of the entire work. After telling how it "came to pass" that a diverse group of people, "from all parts of the earth," had assembled on the common, Giovannitti writes in Biblical form:

Blessed are the strong in freedom's spirit: for theirs is the kingdom of the earth.

Blessed are they that mourn their martyred dead: for they shall avenge them upon their murderers and be comforted.

Blessed are they which do hunger and thirst after equality: for they shall eat fruit of their labor . . .

Blessed are they which are persecuted for equality's sake: for theirs is the glory of the brotherhood of man.

Blessed are ye when the scribes of the press shall revile you, and the doctors of the law, politicians policemen, judges and priests shall call you criminals, thieves and murderers shall say all manner of evil against you falsely, for the sake of justice . . .

The message of Giovannitti's sermon is not one of passive waiting and perseverance—as is often implicit in Jesus' sermon—but a revolutionary credo of action. He urges the working class: "Do not moan, do not submit, do not kneel, do not pray, do not wait—Think, dare, do, rebel, fight—ARISE!" And with the rise of the working class and the demise of the capitalist "man-beast," writes the poet, "the bloody chronicle of the brute shall cease and the story of man shall begin." Although the poem closes with the working class savior apparently vanquished, his closing words to the masses offer a ray of hope before the forces of darkness, the legions of "law and order" and "sacred institutions" set in:

> Through you, by the power of your brain and hand,
>   All the predictions of the prophets,
>   All the wisdom of the sages,
>   All the dreams of the poets,
>   All the hopes of the heroes,
>   All the visions of the martyrs,
>   All the prayers of the saints,
> All the crushed, tortured, strangled, maimed and murdered ideals of the ages, and all the glorious destinies of mankind shall become a triumphant and everlasting reality in the name of labor and bread love, the great three-fold truth forever
> And lo and behold, my brothers, this shall be called the revolution.[66]

Like most sectarians, Giovannitti argues in his poetry that the values of the culturally dominant churches have gone far astray from the "pure" Christian values. The I.W.W., like Giovannitti himself, "rejects the social environment in which it exists" and its creeds while espousing the values of "pure" revolutionary Christianity. In Giovannitti's introduction to *Arrows in the Gale*, for instance, the opening stanza rejects any conventional adherence to creed, asserting that the poems of this collection resemble not so much an advocacy of a "covenant or pledge" as they do blows of the poet's sledge against the walls of his own cell.

When the publication *Current Opinion* reprinted this poem in their article, "Voices of the Living Poets," (Vol. 57, July-December, 1914), they chose to omit one of the seven stanzas. In this missing stanza, Giovannitti asserts the need for workers to fight their own battles rather than complacently affirm that a crucifixion has brought salvation for the people:

> I stand a watch at the van post of my own war I'm captain of,
> No holy fire of pentecost can force on me a savior's love.
> I fight alone and win or sink I need no one to make me free,
> I want no Jesus Christ to think that he could ever die for me.[67]

This stanza, deemed too controversial to include in a liberal publication like *Current Opinion*, rejects not Christ but rather the idea that his sacrifice, made nearly two thousand years ago, can be substituted for the struggles and sacrifices of workers today.

Jesus Christ, for Giovannitti and the other Wobbly poets, was a rebel not unlike the rebels and martyrs of their own struggles, who died for the working class of his day like Joe Hill and Wesley Everest were to die for the same class two thousand years later. In "The Stranger at the Gate," for example, Giovannitti tells of a rootless wanderer who asks the gatekeeper (undoubtedly, of the city of Jerusalem) for information about "the man ye crucified yesterday." As the poem progresses, the stranger learns that among the offenses the crucified man had been charged with were offending the "godliness of our supreme law," pitying "the poor and the lowly," mingling with "the rabble" and, most offensive of all, believing "in a new religion, contrary to the established church."[68] Only through the struggles of the working class, Giovannitti believed, could the religion of the ruling class (institution of the church) be converted into a religion of the disinherited. As he says to the working class in "The Revolution," a poem written for the Labor Pageant, held by the Rand School of Social Science in New York, it is only through the organized strength of the working class that "religion shall become truth."[69]

In his *New Masses* article on the Wobblies' role in American literature, Alan Calmer dubs Ralph Chaplin, along with Giovannitti, "the ablest of the minor poets around the I.W.W."[70] Although best known for his widely hailed labor anthem, "Solidarity Forever," Ralph Chaplin (1887–1961), as unquestionably one of the most prolific poets and songwriters of the I.W.W., appeared often in the pages of the Wobbly press as artist, poet, and editor of such publications as *Solidarity* and the *IW*.[71] Beginning his radical apprenticeship in the Socialist Party of America in 1901, Chaplin joined the I.W.W. in 1913, went to prison with numerous other Wobbly leaders in 1918, joined the Communist Party briefly in the 1920's, and landed in the arms of the Roman Catholic Church in the 1950's.[72] Carl Sandburg, in his April 14, 1956, letter to novelist James T. Farrell, wondered why "Ralph Chaplin, the sturdy, Wobbly poet, has taken shelter under the Catholic Church."[73]

An attempted answer to Sandburg's query might shed some light on the Wobbly poets generally as well as on the impetus for their poetry and the character of their sectarianism. As illustrated by the poems of Chaplin cited earlier, and as Calmer points out in his article, the best of Wobbly poetry dealt with their fallen heroes. Martyrdom, in the eyes of the Wobbly press, is an inevitable, if tragic, result of heroic class struggle. And as V. D. Scudder had said and the Wobbly press was fond of quoting, "Great literature is always the record of some great struggle."[74] It is not surprising that, with the exception of Covington Hall, all of the Wobbly poets discussed in this chapter are "prison poets," members of the I.W.W. who produced a good deal of their work while confined in prison. "Ralph Chaplin was guilty of the most serious social offense that a man can commit," says Scott Nearing in his introduction to Chaplin's prison poems, *Bars and Shadows*:

While living in an old and shattered social order, he had championed a new order of society and had expounded a new culture. Socrates and Jesus, for like offenses, lost their lives. Thousands of their followers, guilty of no greater crime than that of denouncing vested wrong and expounding truths, have suffered in dungeon, on the scaffold and at the stake.[75]

Conflict, struggle and protest were essential elements in maintaining the strength and solidarity of the sect. When protest gives way to reconciliation, says Liston Pope in his influential work, *Millhands and Preachers*, the sect begins the transformation Pope sees as inevitable: the transformation from the "sect type" to the "church type" of organization. For a sect to remain a sect—to continue as what Weber calls a "community of personal believers of the reborn"—it must remain a protest form against the traditional order of things.[76] For the I.W.W. poets, "every new conflict evoked some kind of poetic response." As Calmer correctly points out:

Joe Hill was in the thick of the Wobbly struggles to the very end. It is significant to point out that both Ralph Chaplin and Arturo Giovannitti . . . stopped writing when they withdrew from the forefront of the labor conflict. Their well of inspiration apparently ran dry once they lost contact with the revolutionary vanguard.[77]

Stated in other terms, when these poets lost their feeling of solidarity with the disinherited, they cast their lot with the more socially acceptable forces. For Giovannitti, it was a reactionary section of the labor movement[78] and for Chaplin it was the Catholic church.

The two remaining poets, Charles Ashleigh and Covington Hall, maintained their allegiance to the forces of protest, refusing to join hands with the proponents of the *status quo*. Ashleigh (1892–   ) came to the United States from England in 1910. Joining the I.W.W. a year later, Ashleigh became a prominent organizer, writer and eventually a "class war prisoner."[79] Like Ralph Chaplin, Ashleigh was victimized by the "red scare" hysteria in America following the Bolshevik Revolution of November 1917, and, in the Chicago trial of 1918, was sentenced, along with Bill Haywood and others, to heavy fines and long prison terms.[80] While Chaplin merely said, upon receiving his twenty-year sentence, "I am proud I climbed high enough for the lightening to strike me,"[81] Ashleigh described the scene in words of solidarity and triumph:

When the verdict came, we bore ourselves proudly as kings in the exalted dignity of a cause that knows no defeat—the cause of the working class. Just think of labor, powerful yet blind, stumbling, fumbling, hesitating—yet slowly awakening to its historic mission: that of fighting in the world-wide arena of the class struggle, for the freedom of the whole world.[82]

Four years earlier, in his article in *The Little Review*, Ashleigh described the importance of this sense of struggle to the creative process. In praising the poetry of Giovannitti, for example, he asserts that the reason for the higher quality of the poetry is that "Giovannitti has realized the pregnant fact that in struggle is the greatest joy, that the ecstasy of growth and striving is worth more than the bovine placidity of happiness."

In a later issue of the *Review*, Ashleigh confesses "a certain disappointment" in John Galsworthy's new play, "The Mob." In the play, an upper-class statesman, Sir Stephen More, is killed by a mob for protesting, on pacifistic grounds, the war of conquest which his country is carrying out against a small nation. Besides objecting to the heroic depiction of More, "who belongs to the class which really benefits by war: the monied, aristocratic and governing class," Ashleigh objects to the pacifist grounds for opposing war. Holding to the sectarian belief in the unifying function of protest and struggle, Ashleigh writes that "a great, popular, full-blooded thing like war must have a great, popular, full-blooded thing to counteract it." Later in the same article, Ashleigh writes that "the spirit of conflict is good, it is essential to continuity, it is the breaker of old forms and the releaser of new life." As to the working class opposing capitalist wars, Ashleigh says:

If the people, the mass of producers are to stop war, they must first be stirred; and a negative pacifist preaching will never stir them. Only a call to a greater and more vital war can move them.[83]

Such a war was the notorious "Everett Massacre" in Washington state on November 5, 1916.[84] After nearly six months of trying to win free speech in this Washington town, three hundred Wobblies sailed from Seattle to Everett in two steamboats, the *Verona* and the *Calista*. Confident that their demonstration would result in victory, the Wobblies landed the *Verona* in high spirits, singing "Hold the Fort" and other songs. To their horror, the *Verona* was immediately fired upon by policemen and armed vigilantes who were trying to prevent their landing.[85] The tragic result: five workers and two vigilantes dead, thirty-one workers and nineteen vigilantes wounded, and seven workers missing, probably drowned.[86]

The poem which Charles Ashleigh, publicity agent for the Everett Defense Committee, wrote in commemoration of the massacre, "Everett, November Fifth," puts into poetic form the concepts of struggle and art that he presents in his *Little Review* articles. It captures well the joy of conflict combined with the tragedy of martyrhood and the psychology of persecution.[87] The poem, occasioned by a witness's account of a Wobbly falling to his death with the words of "Hold the Fort" on his lips, first appeared in the February 1917 issue of the *International Socialist Review*. The rousing refrain illustrates the joy which the class-struggle soldiers felt as they marched to do battle with the forces of evil:

> Song on his lips, he came;
> Song on his lips, he went;—
> This be the token we bear of him—
> Soldier of Discontent.

In the first stanza, we read that the "soldiers of discontent" march bravely into the class battle with "flaming hope" and "every heart aglow." There is no thought of Debsian conciliation as the "soldiers" move forward to battle, "bare hands against the masters' armored might."

Sects, which proliferate in periods of social unrest,[88] often adopt, as mentioned earlier, a "psychology of persecution" to instill its members with a sense of solidarity and battle-readiness.[89] This characteristic appears in apocalyptic proportions in the last stanza of Ashleigh's poem, as the army of labor finds itself face to face with the Satanic army of capitalism which paints the deck of the *Verona* red as they "spewed shots and mockery." But the dying worker proves himself heroic—personal merit being an important characteristic for the sect[90]—as he maintains his song of triumph even in the face of certain death:

> Yet the mad chorus from the devil's host,—
> Yea, all the tumult of that butcher throng,—
> Compound of bullets, booze and coward boast,—
> Could not out-shriek one dying worker's song!

In that song—"Hold the Fort" (no doubt Chaplin's version, discussed in Chapter 3)—the scene of battle is transported to Armageddon where "the final battle rages" and "tyrants quake with fear." Here the revolutionary unionist—the "soldiers of discontent"—are being called to "a greater and more vital war" than the one the capitalists have created in Europe: it is the class war depicted apocalyptically in both Chaplin's songs and Ashleigh's poem.

In the poetry of Covington Hall—particularly his *Songs of Love and Rebellion* (1915)—the class war remains in Armageddon where it takes on a more distinctly metaphysical coloring than in the works of the previously discussed Wobbly poets. The distinctions between church and sect, institutional and prophetic religion, harmony and rebellion that were often implicit in the poetry of Hill, Giovannitti, Chaplin and Ashleigh become quite explicit in much of the poetry of Covington Hall (1871–1951).

Although the only one of the five who was not a "prison poet," Hall was certainly not isolated from the thick of the battle. Born in Mississippi, the son of a Presbyterian minister and a wealthy southern belle, Hall was instrumental in organizing the "timber beasts" and bringing the message of the Wobblies to the South.[91] When the Brotherhood of Timber Workers, founded in June of 1911 and initially only tenuously linked to the I.W.W., began to adopt conservative Southern attitudes toward race, violence, employers, and class conflict, Bill Haywood went south in 1912, accompanied by Covington Hall, to attend the union's second regional convention (May 6–9). After both men presented their impassioned, militant pleas, the union voted to affiliate formally with the I.W.W. and to adopt a more revolutionary constitution.[92]

In the midst of the BTW's struggle to purge the conservative elements from its ranks and to fight the lumber barons of Louisiana and Texas in the strike of 1911–12, Hall wrote his frequently reprinted poem, "Us the Hoboes and Dreamers." Written three or four years before *Songs*, this work captures the prophetic tone of the later poems and illustrates dramatically the joy of struggle Ashleigh found in the poetry of Giovannitti, particularly in the first and last stanzas. As the poem opens, the rebel voice declares that the class struggle transcends the parochial boundaries of southern culture, scorning the feudalistic "power that now holds the south in awe." The forces of proletarian rebellion, says Hall, shall "trample on your customs," spit upon southern law and, in defiance against the religion of capitalism, shall "outrage all your temples" and "blaspheme all your gods."[93]

In the "rebellion" section of *Songs of Love and Rebellion*, Hall continues the blasphemous tone of the earlier poem, but this time it is on the loftier plane of William Blake's prophetic poetry, reminiscent of Los's utterance in "Jerusalem" that "I must create a system, or be enslav'd by another Man's." (Plate 10, Line 20) Although it would be difficult and well beyond the scope of this study to determine how extensively Hall was influenced by the prophetic books of Blake (it would be hard to imagine he did not read them), Marxist critic Fred Whitehead's remark on Blake's poetry could as easily be applied to Hall's *Songs*: "Writing in the radical chiliastic tradition, he believed that the Bible provided important clues concerning the historical origins of ancient man, as well as indications of the kind of revolutionary transformation needed to overcome the tragic paradigms of class society."[94]

Like Blake, Hall creates a Biblical universe in order to make critical comments about his society. For Hall, such figures as Jesus, Lucifer, Jehovah, Calvin and the Virgin Mary all play an important symbolic role in evoking the Gospel of Rebellion. An examination of the role that these characters play reveals much of the cosmology of I.W.W. poetry in general. As with the other four poets discussed, a clear distinction emerges in Hall's work between the rebel heroes of the disinherited—"soldiers of discontent"—and the oppressive forces of the church, denomination or institution.

The appropriate opening poem, "Rebellion," sets the tone for all the poems that follow.[95] In the first two stanzas, the virtue of rebellion is introduced, along with its chief proponents and opponents, in language that Wobbly writers reserve only for such "sacred" traits as this, or the sister-virtue of "solidarity":

> Rebellion comes, hope's sacred fire,
> To Freedom's son from Freedom's sire,
> A soul-breath swordsmen cannot kill,
> Nor gold, nor cross, nor rifle still.
>
> With Lucifer it marched on God
> And broke Jehovah's scourging rod:
> It stood with Christ in Pilate's hall
> And doomed the Caesars to their fall. (p. 3)

For Covington Hall, as for William Blake, Lucifer and Christ represent the qualities of rebellion, while the Old Testament God, Jehovah, appears as an authoritarian figure like Pilate and the Caesars.[96] In Hall's "Lucifer, the Morning Star," one finds the qualities that were appealing to Milton and Blake in earlier periods, and to a revolutionary poet in the twentieth century:

> He was the first to face the wrath of priesthoods and of kings;
> He was the first to make his mind the judgement-place of things;
> He was the first to question, first to feel the steel of might—
> Lucifer, the Morning Star, the splendid and the bright!

In the last stanza, Hall sums up his reason for such veneration in the words—"Hail to the first of rebels!" Lucifer, hurled from Paradise by an authoritarian Old Testament God is, for Hall, as much a rebel in the Old Testament world as Christ, throwing the moneychangers out of the temple, is in the New Testament world. In "Jesus Christ," Hall follows the path of much Wobbly poetry by equating the cause and martyrhood of Jesus with the cause of labor. In the second stanza, Hall writes:

> On the cross they built for labor, lo! they hanged you in the night;
> And the jeering preachers cheered it as a deed for good and right;
> But the workers gathered 'round you, and the Revolution spread;
> And the priesthood and the masters for a moment were afraid.
>   (p. 13)

The figure of Jehovah, for Hall, has none of the ambiguity of Blake's Old Testament God. Rather, it is a purely tyrannical figure, equivalent to the tyranny of the organized church. In Hall's bitterly ironic poem, "In God We Trust," the poem begins with this scathing stanza:

> In God we trust—the God of Gold,
> The fiend Jehovah, hard and cold;
> The merciless, supreme Unjust—
> The God of slaves—in Him we trust. (p. 7)

It is this tyrannical God, Hall feels, that the organized church worships. Orthodox Christianity, for Hall as well as Blake, "was not merely a corruption of Christianity . . . but its absolute inversion."[97] While Blake asserts that the "Modern Church Crucifies Christ with the head Downward,"[98] Hall charges that the modern church invariably "will crown a Constantine and cheer a Calvin on his way." (p. 7) He also writes, in "The Church":

> The church fights never fairly, never on the open plain,
> But tigerlike and stealthily, with dagger, dirk and chain;
> Up through the gloom of ignorance, unseen, unheard, felt-shod,
> It creeps upon its victim, and strikes in the name of God. (p. 7)

In the final poem of his *Songs of Rebellion*, entitled "The World Will," Hall makes a final battle cry for the working class before he slips into the often embarassing sentimentalism of his

Songs of Love. In the last stanza of this poem, one finds qualities—sectarianism, prophecy, rebellion—that characterize the bulk of Wobbly poetry which has been examined in this chapter. In contrast to the closing message of Chaplin's autobiography, which calls for "a collaboration with God's universal law" and "a revitalized American ideology,"[99] Hall chooses unflinchingly the path of rebellion rather than civil religion. One might say that after the martyrhood of Hill, Little and Everest; Giovannitti's "Sermon on the Common"; and Ashleigh's proclamation on the sacred conflict of the class struggle, the last stanza of Hall's poem points the way toward proletarian salvation:

> There shall be no king above us, there shall be no slave below,
> There, in Labor's Grand Republic, only freedom we shall know!
> We are gathering, we are coming, far and wide the world around,
> Truth the northstar of our legions, all the earthy our battle-
>   ground!
> Arming, coming hungry-hearted for the long expected fight!
> Coming, coming from our thralldom, coming victors over all!—
> We have heard the World Will speaking, we have heard the
>   Race-Soul call! (p. 16)

NOTES

1. Herbert Mitgang, ed. *The Letters of Carl Sandburg* (New York: Harcourt, Brace and World, 1968), p. 108.

2. Ralph Chaplin, *Wobbly: The Rough-and-Tumble Story of an American Radical* (Chicago: University of Chicago Press, 1948), p. 98.

3. Amos N. Wilder, *The Spiritual Aspects of the New Poetry* (New York: Harper and Brothers Publishers, 1940), p. 221.

4. Wilder, *Spiritual Aspects of the New Poetry*, p. 38.

5. Ralph Chaplin, *Bars and Shadows: The Prison Poems of Ralph Chaplin* (New York: The Leonard Press, 1922), pp. 10–11.

6. Henry F. May, *The End of American Innocence: A Study of the First Years of Our Own Time, 1912–1917* (New York: Knopf, 1959), p. 249.

7. Ibid.

8. Genevieve Taggard, ed., *May Days: An Anthology of Verse from Masses-Liberator [1912–1924]* (New York: Boni and Liveright, 1925), p. 14.

9. Patrick Renshaw, *The Wobblies: The Story of Syndicalism in*

the United States (New York: Anchor Books-Doubleday, 1967), p. 14.

10. Melvyn Dubofsky, *We Shall Be All: A History of the I.W.W.* (New York: Quadrangle Press, 1969), p. 308.

11. Dean Nolan and Fred Thompson, *Joe Hill: I.W.W. Songwriter* (Chicago: Industrial Workers of the World, 1979), p. 4. The date of Hill's birth is disputed among historians, Foner and Dubofsky have him born in 1879 while Kornbluh and Renshaw accept Ralph Chaplin's date of 1882. (Chaplin, *Wobbly*, p. 185)

12. Joyce L. Kornbluh, ed. *Rebel Voices: An I.W.W. Anthology* (Ann Arbor: University of Michigan Press, 1964), pp. 127–132.

13. George Milburn, *The Hobo's Hornbook: A Repertory for a Gutter Jongleur* (New York: Ives Washburn, 1930), p. 117.

14. Ibid., pp. 131–132.

15. May, *End of American Innocence*, p. 178.

16. Nolan and Thompson, *Joe Hill: I.W.W. Songwriter*, p. 5.

17. Dubofsky, pp. 147 and 169.

18. Georges Sorel, *Reflections on Violence* (New York: The Free Press, 1950), p. 187.

19. *Solidarity*, June 27, 1914, p. 2.

20. Alan Calmer, "The Wobbly in American Literature," *New Masses* (September 18, 1934), p. 22.

21. Gibbs M. Smith, *Joe Hill* (Salt Lake City: University of Utah Press, 1969), p. 91.

22. Elizabeth Gurley Flynn, *The Rebel Girl: An Autobiography* (New York: International Publishers, 1955), p. 192.

23. Smith, *Joe Hill*, p. 176.

24. Calmer, p. 21.

25. Sorel, p. 184.

26. Smith, p. 192.

27. Renshaw, *Wobblies*, p. 163.

28. Reprinted in Kornbluh's *Rebel Voices*, p. 275.

29. Liston Pope, *Millhands and Preachers: A Study of Gastonia* (New Haven and London: Yale University Press, 1942), p. 123.

30. Ibid., p. 118.

31. Max Weber, *The Protestant Ethic and the Spirit of Capitalism* (New York: Charles Scribner's Sons, 1958), p. 145.

32. Kornbluh, p. 156.

33. A provocative symposium on this debate, entitled "Church-Sect Reappraised," appears in the Spring 1967, issue of the *Journal for the Scientific Study of Religion*. Here Paul Gustafson, Erich Goode, N. J. Demerath, and Allan Eister debate the value of the church-sect typology.

34. Benton Johnson, "On Church and Sect," *American Sociological Review* 28, 4 (August 1963), p. 542.

35. Sidney E. Ahlstom, *A Religious History of the American People* (New Haven and London: Yale University Press, 1972), p. 473.

36. Ibid., pp. 799–800.

37. Dubofsky, pp. 63–64.

38. Philip S. Foner, *The Industrial Workers of the World, 1905–1917* (New York: International Publishers, 1965), pp. 326–328 and Dubofsky, pp. 350–352.

39. Notably, Foner offers two chapters on Lawrence in his book ("The Lawrence Strike" and "Victory at Lawrence and After") and Dubofsky devotes a sizable chapter to the strike (Satan's Dark Mills: Lawrence, 1912).

40. Foner, pp. 340–343.

41. Walter Weyl, "The Lawrence Strike from Various Angles," *Survey* 28, 1 (April 1912), pp. 65–80.

42. Kornbluh, p. 127; Dubofsky, p. 190.

43. Smith, *Joe Hill*, p. 27.

44. Foner, p. 333.

45. Flynn, p. 150.

46. Dubofsky, p. 256; Foner, p. 348.

47. Flynn, p. 151.

48. Ibid., p. 150.

49. Foner, p. 349.

50. Smith, p. 27.

51. Charles Ashleigh, "The Poetry of Revolt," *The Little Review* 1, 6 (September 1914), p. 22.

52. Justus Ebert, "Arturo Giovannitti," *Industrial Worker* (May 30, 1912), pp. 1 and 4.

53. "The Poetry of Syndicalism," *Atlantic Monthly* 3 (June 1913), pp. 853–854.

54. Ibid.

55. Arturo Giovannitti, *Arrow in the Gale*, intro. by Helen Keller (Riverside, Connecticut: Hillacre Bookhouse, 1914), pp. 9–10.

56. "Voices of the Living Poets," *Current Opinion* 57 (July-December 1914), p. 54.

57. Kenneth MacGowan, "Giovannitti: Poet of the Wobblies," *The Forum* 52 (October 1914), p. 610.

58. Benton Johnson, "On Church and Sect," p. 541.

59. This generational warfare can be seen, more recently, in much of the rhetoric, poetry and music of the so-called "Youth Generation" of the 1960's.

60. Foner, p. 336.

61. Quotations from "The Cage," appear in *The Collected Poems of Arturo Giovannitti* (p. 206) from which all quotations of Giovannitti's poetry are taken unless otherwise noted.

62. Ashleigh, p. 23.

63. MacGowan, p. 611.

64. Benton Johnson, p. 542.

65. Flynn, p. 128.

66. Giovannitti, "Sermon on the Common," *Collected Poems*, p. 193.

67. Giovannitti, "Proem," p. 144.

68. Giovannitti, "The Stranger at the Gate," *Arrows in the Gale*, pp. 31–34.

69. *Survey* 36 (June 24, 1916), p. 335.

70. Calmer, p. 22.

71. Kornbluh, p. 26.

72. Biographical notations in the index to Renshaw's *Wobblies*, p. 245. Chaplin's story is told in his autobiography, *Wobbly*.

73. Sandburg, *Letters*, pp. 509–510.

74. Calmer, p. 21.

75. Chaplin, *Bars and Shadows*, p. 6. Nearing was the radical organizer for the anti-war People's Council of America for Peace and Democracy (see Symes' and Clement's *Rebel America: The Story of Social Revolt in the United States* (Boston: Beacon Press, 1972), p. 299.

76. Pope's *Millhands*, p. 118 and Weber's *Protestant Ethic*, p. 145.

77. Calmer, pp. 21–22.

78. Ibid., p. 22.

79. Kornbluh, p. 79.

80. Renshaw, p. 186.

81. Chaplin, *Wobbly*, p. 247.

82. Ibid., p. 187.

83. Ashleigh, "The Poetry of Revolt," *Little Review*, p. 24 and "New Wars for Old," *LR* 1, 7 (October 1914), pp. 11–12.

84. Foner includes an entire chapter on the "massacre," and Kornbluh twenty-one pages to the tragedy, including Walker C. Smith's excellent summary, "The Voyage of the Verona," as well as the Ashleigh poem and a few devastating cartoons from the Wobbly Press.

85. Renshaw, p. 93.

86. Walker C. Smith, "The Voyage of the Verona," reprinted in Kornbluh, pp. 107–112.

87. The poem was first published in the February 1917, issue of the *International Socialist Review* and was frequently reprinted, including (in part) in Foner's book (p. 548) and completely in Kornbluh's (pp. 106–107).

88. Bryan R. Wilson, "An Analysis of Sect Development," in Wil-

liam M. Newman's *The Social Meaning of Religion* (Chicago: Rand McNally, 1974), p. 259.

89. Pope, p. 123.

90. Wilson, p. 251.

91. Kornbluh, pp. 259–260.

92. Dubofsky, pp. 211–212 and p. 216. Chapter 9 of *We Shall Be All* deals with the little discussed subject of I.W.W. organizing in the South.

93. First appearing in *Rebellion* (June 1916), the poem is reprinted in Kornbluh, p. 260.

94. Fred Whitehead, "William Blake and Radical Tradition," *Weapons of Criticism: Marxism in America and the Literary Tradition*, ed. by Norman Rudich (Palo Alto, California: Ramparts Press, 1976), p. 195.

95. Parenthetical page numbers following the poems all refer to *Songs of Love and Rebellion* by Covington Hall (New Orleans: Weihing Printing Co., 1915).

96. J. Bronowski, *William Blake and the Age of Revolution* (New York: Harper and Row, 1965), p. 12.

97. A. L. Morton, *The Everlasting Gospel: A Study in the Source of William Blake* (London: Lawrence and Wisehart, 1958), p. 49.

98. Ibid.

99. Chaplin, *Wobbly*, pp. 426–427.

6

Wobbly Direct Action, Finnish Protestantism, and the Mesabi Range Strike of 1916

In 1916, while the Wobblies sang zealously of the holy class war, the world's rulers were preparing for another type of conflict. The question of whether or not America should become involved in the European War was one of the major issues of the 1916 Presidential campaign between Democrat Woodrow Wilson, Republican Charles E. Hughes, and Socialist A. L. Benson. Although most Americans still opposed intervention, the manufacturing interests, who had extended huge amounts of credit to the Allies, pushed vigorously for war. "American industry and finance," write Symes and Clement in *Rebel America*, "could no longer afford to have the Allies lose." Nevertheless, during the same period "when industry was humming with Allied war orders," the vast number of strikes throughout America "nearly drove the war news from the front pages of the daily papers."[1]

The Industrial Workers of the World, who believed strongly that the class war at home should take priority over the military conflict in Europe, provided "a tremendous spiritual impetus to the progressive movement." The Wobbly-led strikes "revealed how thoroughly industry controlled local governments, and how willing it was to use its control with brutal ferocity that gave no regard to civil rights."[2] One strike where this revelation emerged clearly and where the I.W.W. provided a great "spiritual impetus" to an immigrant community was the Iron Range strike in Minnesota.

"The strike of the iron miners of Minnesota in 1916," writes Bill Haywood in his autobiography, "was a great event in the history of the Industrial Workers of the World."[3] While seen as a failure by most historians, the Mesabi Range strike and the events surrounding it yielded many positive results for the Wobblies. In addition to the eventual improvement of working conditions in the mines which the strike helped to win, a vigorous spirit of labor solidarity emerged among the predominantly Finnish workers on the Range—thanks largely to the organizing efforts of the I.W.W. The radical socialists among the Finns, greatly impressed by the lessons in class struggle they had learned partially from the Wobbly organizers during the strike, even transformed their newspaper, *Socialisti*, into an I.W.W. organ.[4]

What appeal did the I.W.W. have for the immigrant workers on the Mesabi Range? Why did the Finns in particular—numerically the strongest and politically the most influential[5]—find the ideology of the I.W.W. attractive? How was the I.W.W. tactic of "direct action," particularly as it was applied in the 1916 strike, compatible with the Finnish culture generally and with conflicting elements or tendencies within that culture specifically, such as anarchism and Finnish Protestantism? Such questions can be better answered after one acquires some understanding, first, of immigrant (particularly Finnish) experience on the Mesabi Range and, second, of the I.W.W.'s efforts to recruit Finnish workers by preaching the "gospel" of class struggle and direct action, and by demonstrating the effectiveness of these ideas in the 1916 strike itself.

A large percentage of the Finnish immigrants and migrants, between the period of 1864 to the first World War, located themselves in the Western Great Lakes region. In the year 1900, the Federal Census determined that 50.8 percent of the total of 62,641 Finns which they tabulated, lived in Wisconsin, Michigan or Minnesota.[6] And most of the first wave of Finnish immigrants found themselves working in mines since, as Matti E. Kaups points out and proves in his paper on Finnish settlement in the iron ore region, "the arrival of the Finns in the summer of 1864 was directly related to manpower shortage in the mines brought about by the Civil War [in America]."[7] With the opening of the iron mines on the Range, in the year 1891 and thereafter, Finns flocked to Northeastern Minnesota in such large numbers that, by 1905, they were the largest of the foreign-born groups on the Range, comprising 39.8 percent of the total foreign-born population of 14,923.[8] And, according to the U.S. Immigration Commission figures, the average annual salary of foreign-born workers on the Mesabi was $644 in 1909, compared with $981 for native-born workers.[9]

From their earliest days on the North American continent, the Finnish immigrants sought to place their own unique cultural stamp upon the settlements they established. New institutions, associations and activities began to emerge in Northern Minnesota that were conspicuously Finnish and that knitted the community together in ethnic solidarity. Band and choral music societies flourished, temperance halls were built in almost every Finnish community, churches were established, newspapers were published, and the often-celebrated "Finn Hall," writes Carl Ross in *The Finn Factor*, became "the extraordinary institution of Finnish immigrant life that served as their cultural, associational, and political center through succeeding years."[10]

In 1890, the Suomi Synod, or Finnish Evangelical Lutheran Church, was established, modeling itself on the state church in Finland, and appearing at about the same time as the "Workingmen's Societies" began to appear.[11]

Evangelical Lutheranism and proletarian consciousness, though usually at odds with each other, possessed often-ignored elements of compatibility that produced a unique variety of radicalism in the Finnish communities on the Mesabi Range. In his article on the Suomi Synod and socialism, Arthur E. Puotinen points out that, despite the many areas of tension between socialists and ministers, within what he sees as a three-class socio-economic division, "most American Finns in the mining regions before W.W. I. stood in [the] lower class" from which most Synod pastors came. Thus in the context of this class continuity, ministers could sometimes be pressured by workers into supporting strikes. In his "Reflections on a Strike," in the 1913 issues of *American Suometar* (American

Finn), Pastor B. William Rautanen of the Suomi Synod congregation in Calumet defended the copper strike as legal and called for the company to recognize the Western Federation of Miners.[12]

Another social issue of common concern to both the churches and the workers' societies was the matter of temperance. "Under the umbrella of the temperance societies and generally in the same halls," Ross writes, "these newly awakened concerns about social issues crystallized in a movement of working people's clubs, while the proponents of religious salvation launched a more highly organized and successful church effort."[13]

Like the Wobblies and the Salvation Army in the Western free-speech struggles between 1909 and 1912, the churches and the workers' organizations were competing for the same audience among the Finnish community. Since there was no actual social gospel movement in the Finnish culture, where religious beliefs and the need for social reform might meet on a common ground, religious and secular programs frequently found themselves engaged in ideological warfare. Nevertheless, in the midst of this conflict was a value held by almost all Finnish immigrants, regardless of their associational ties: a distrust of excessive power. Suspicious of clergymen and the possibility of domination of daily life by a state church, as they had known in Finland, the Finnish people tended toward sect formation rather than reliance upon a powerful, national church organization.[14]

Since an immigrant society tends to be individualistic,[15] and since the Finnish laypersons viewed church authority with suspicion, it was less than unusual that the religious emphasis in the Finnish community shifted from faith in institutional religion to the belief in a religion of personal searching and striving.[16] Finnish Protestantism, by virtue of its anticlerical and individualistic nature, "transcends the walls of cathedrals, churches and meeting houses and becomes part of the culture."[17]

Like the churches, the Finnish workers' organizations were also suspicious of centralized authority. Initially, these organizations were decidedly non-socialist, advocating nationalism rather than radicalism, self-help activity rather than trade-union activism.[18] But events in the Finnish community and on the international scene had a radicalizing effect on these organizations. In the early years of the twentieth century, a number of mine disasters across the country resulted in the deaths of numerous Finnish workers. Most notably, in early 1900, a mine explosion in Utah cost 325 coal miners their lives, 63 of them Finns; and three years later, in Wyoming, the majority of the 169 workers killed in a mine disaster there were Finnish.[19] These events, coupled with the impact of the Russian Revolution of 1905, had a radicalizing influence on the Finnish workers' organizations.

In August of 1906, delegates from the workers' clubs gathered in Hibbing, Minnesota, to found the Finnish Socialist Federation, which quickly grew from 2,450 members at its organizational meeting to about 11,000 members by 1912.[20] By the following year, the founder of the Range parish, Rev. William J. Bell, estimated that one-third of the Finns on the Range were socialists.[21]

The 1906 Hibbing convention was certainly "one of the most important events to occur in the history of the Finnish ethnic group in America."[22] After Kaapo Murros, the fiery Finnish militant and editor of *Tyomies* (The Workman), gave a support speech for the I.W.W., the delegates passed a resolution proclaiming that "unions in America that grope for bourgeois approval" are the opponents of working people, and that unions grounded in class struggle and socialism are the only ones worth supporting. After a good deal of debate, the delegates also passed a resolution dealing with "The Question of Religion." The strongly anti-clerical resolution called for opposition to "any religion which is counterproductive to the class struggle" and for support for any "natural religion" that does not infringe on the freedom or rights of the individual as long as such a religion remains a "personal matter."[23]

Although often in conflict with each other over central beliefs and attitudes, the Finnish churches and the workers' organizations, including the Finnish Socialist Federation, frequently found themselves meeting on a common territory.

Significantly, the rank-and-file of both groups often shared similar ideas about the I.W.W., anarchism, morality and direct action—all major issues in the 1916 strike.

Following the disastrous defeat of the 1907 strike on the Mesabi Range, the members of the Finnish Socialist Federation engaged in a vigorous debate at their 1909 convention about the form that their struggle against capitalism generally, and the mining companies specifically, should take. In response to the conservative Finns who opposed "disruptive radicalism," the Federation passed a resolution condemning anarchy and denying that "self-conscious anarchy . . . has been observed even in small measures in the . . . Finnish Socialist Federation."[24] Nevertheless, although they stopped short of endorsing the I.W.W., the convention took a favorable stand on industrial unionism, direct economic action, the general strike, and the relegation of religion to the realm of private belief.[25]

One might wonder why the I.W.W. became an issue at the Federation's 1909 convention if, as most historians contend, the Wobblies played no role in the Mesabi Range previous to the 1916 strike. Neil Betten in his article in *Minnesota History* asserts that by 1916 the I.W.W. had "made no effort to organize the workers of Northern Minnesota."[26] Mr. Betten, like most historians who have written of the strike, is incorrect in his assessment of the length of I.W.W. influence or attempted organization on the Range. Shortly after the ideology of the I.W.W. became a regular topic of discussion among the Finns—in the 1909 Federation convention and in the statements of Yrjo Sirola, an influential Moscow Finn who came to America in 1910—the Wobblies had direct contact with the Mesabi Range.[27]

In 1913, Wobbly agitators Frank Little, James Cannon, and E. F. Doree came to Duluth with the intention of moving north and west to the Range communities, recruiting immigrant workers as they went. But in August, a group of Duluth businessmen kidnapped Little in order to send a clear message to the I.W.W. about what was in store for them if they tried intervening in their private, capitalist domain. Although Little was eventually rescued by other Wobblies, this incident convinced the I.W.W. that repression was too great to organize the immigrant miners at that time.[28]

A year later, at the district convention of the Finnish Socialist Federation, the Mesabi Range socialists broke from the national pro-parliamentary, anti-syndicalist body by strongly affirming industrial unionism and giving its stamp of approval to the I.W.W.[29] The Finnish socialists, most of whom were not U.S. citizens (and thus unable to vote) found much more to be favored in the syndicalist, anti-political stance of the Wobblies than in the parliamentarian, moderate socialists.

The Federation's endorsement of the I.W.W. in 1914, motivated in part by the Wobblies' momentous victory in the Lawrence, Massachusetts, textile strike of 1912, was partly an endorsement of the spirit of direct action over the lethargic bureaucracy of Samuel Gompers' A.F.L. This spirit, which emerged visibly in the 1916 strike, was not unlike the emotional energy of revivalistic zeal found in the Finnish churches at this time. David DeLeon, in his recent work, *The American as Anarchist: Reflections on Indigenous Radicalism*, says of the early revivalist movements of the 1720's and 1730's: "although their social perspectives were often conservative, paradoxically added to this anarchist heritage by their appeals to emotion rather than reason and by their creating, through camp meetings, a sense of community without a church."[30]

This comment could provide a clue to why the I.W.W. won broad acceptance among Finnish socialists at a time when the Socialist Party leadership nationally, led by the moderate forces of Morris Hillquit, were excommunicating members that they suspected of supporting what they saw as the "terrorism" and "anarchism" of Big Bill Haywood and other Wobblies.[31] Since both the Finnish churches (at least the majority of their membership) and the Finnish Socialist Federation were in agreement on the role of religion as a private matter, both groups cast their lot with the emotional rather than the institutional function of religion. For, as William Warren Sweet argues, to personalize religion is to emotionalize it.[32] And, unlike the stuffy, armchair socialists of the Hillquit variety, the Industrial Workers of the World—with their irreverent *Little Red*

Songbook, their "propaganda of the deed," and their advocacy of mass action—was a demonstrative movement with a high emotional content.

In the strike of 1916, the pro-company newspapers on the Mesabi Range commercialized on the anarchist reputation of the Wobblies to smear the strikers and attempt to break the strike. Almost from the moment that Joe Greeni, an Italian immigrant miner, walked off the job on June 2, 1916, the Range press, such as the Duluth *News Tribune* and the *Tower News*, were shouting charges of "anarchy" and "sabotage" and accusing the I.W.W. of leaving a trail of blood wherever it went.[33] Since Kornbluh's *Rebel Voices*, Foner's history of the Wobblies, and Dubofsky's *We Shall Be All* deal with the strike in great detail, this study focuses on the little-discussed relationships between the strike and Finnish culture, particularly the "decentralizing" tendencies within that culture on the Mesabi Range.

Although the original walkout by Greeni and others at the St. James mine was spontaneous, the struggle was, undoubtedly, maintained and expanded by the I.W.W. leadership. This is generally accepted by most historians.[34] What is often overlooked, however, is the cultural implications of this Wobbly intervention. In his early work on the Wobblies, *American Syndicalism: The I.W.W.*, John Graham Brooks, in a derogatory manner, discusses the connection between the I.W.W.'s brand of syndicalism and anarchism. "The element of anarchy peculiar to the I.W.W.," he writes, "is its inherent dislike of organic restraint. No one uses the word 'organization' oftener and practices it less." Later, he asserts that "an impetuous individualism cannot endure organic relationships."[35] Brooks, like many hostile critics of I.W.W., confuses "anarchism" with "direct action." Although the Wobblies admittedly borrowed from the anarchist tradition some valuable tactics and principles, it generally rejected individual radical actions, believing, as Elizabeth Gurley Flynn wrote, that "mass action is far more up-to-date than personal or physical violence."[36]

Nevertheless, one of the most effective organizers of the 1916 strike was an anarchist and pacifist editor named George Andreytchine. This Bulgarian clerical worker turned rebel, rejected "personal or physical violence," preached the "gospel" of Tolstoy, Thoreau, and William Lloyd Garrison, and quit his job at the Oliver Mining Company to fight with the I.W.W. in the strike of 1916.[37] In describing Andreytchine, Ralph Chaplin, Wobbly editor and songwriter—composer of the famous "Solidarity Forever"—said of his "brother editor": "George was a handsome young fellow, just twenty-two years old, brilliant, full of life, and a splendid speaker, the idol of all the rebel girls."[38] When Chaplin first met Andreytchine, the Bulgarian anarchist had just returned from the Mesabi Range strike. In his re-telling of the story Andreytchine had related, Chaplin captures in a few words the brutal oppression the Wobblies and Finnish workers experienced on the Range:

He recounted the old story of violence, murder, rape, kidnapping, and imprisonment. Four mine guards attacked the home of unarmed Montenegran miners. One guard killed by the bullets of another. The miners were held for this . . . George Andreytchine . . . was kidnapped, manhandled, and finally turned over to the immigration authorities at Ellis Island.[39]

With such oppressive weapons as these used by the companies against the miners, the Finnish immigrants drew courage from the audacity of the Wobblies in their advocacy of direct action against the consolidated force of capitalism. Direct action, as interpreted and summarized by Dubofsky,

included any steps taken by workers at the point of production which improved wages, reduced hours and bettered conditions. It encompassed conventional strikes, intermittent strikes, silent strikes, passive resistance, sabotage, and the ultimate direct-action measure: the general strike which would displace the capitalists from power.[40]

Such tactics, as pointed out throughout this study, were not without religious significance for the I.W.W. "To strike is divine," says one *Solidarity* editorial written during the Mesabi strike, "only submission is sinful and vile." (5/22/16, p. 2) In opposition to the vile gospel of submission preached by many conservative church Finns—largely those immigrating before 1903, according to Douglas J. Ollila, Jr.—a new Finn was becoming more visible. This "new kind of Finn," says Ollila, "invoked the names of Karl Marx, Robert Ingersoll and Karl Kautsky" and possessed "a new eschatology in the form of the coming great revolution led by the proletariat."[41]

Although Michael Karni, in his dissertation on the Finns, is undoubtedly correct when he asserts that the Finnish community was one divided between the Church-Finns, the temperance-Finns and the Red-Finns,[42] the I.W.W. was in some ways able to bridge this division. By distancing themselves from organized religion and maintaining a "direct action" approach to the struggle on the Iron Range, the I.W.W. allied itself more closely with the sect-forming quality of much of Finnish Protestantism than with the harmonious relationship between socialism and religion that one finds in the American Social Gospel movement.

It was the I.W.W.'s message of direct action together with its concrete examples of this during the strike—massive demonstrations, picket line solidarity, and heroic resistance to the terrorism of the mining companies—that appealed to a broad range of the Finnish community and offered a "spiritual impetus" to the striking miners. The I.W.W., whose ideology ranged from the Tolstoyan anarchism of Andreytchine to the rough-and-tumble syndicalism of Bill Haywood, provided a model of individualism and heroism that inspired both the pre-1917 Finnish socialists and the more activist elements of Finnish revivalism.

NOTES

1. Lillian Symes and Travers Clement, *Rebel America: The Story of Social Revolt in the United States* (Boston: Beacon Press, 1972), pp. 289–290.

2. Joseph A. Rayback, *A History of American Labor* (New York: The Free Press, 1959), p. 249.

3. From the ghost-written autobiography of Haywood, *Bill Haywood's Book* (New York: International Publishers, 1929), p. 290.

4. Melvyn Dubofsky's *We Shall Be All: A History of the I.W.W.* (New York: Quadrangle Press, 1969), p. 331.

5. C. Whit Pfeiffer, "From 'Bohunks' to Finns," *Survey: A Journal of Social Exploration*, 26, 1 (April 1, 1916), p. 13.

6. *Twelfth Census of the U.S., 1900* (Washington: Department of the Interior, 1901), pp. 732–733.

7. Kaups' paper, originally presented at a conference at the University of Minnesota, Duluth, appears in *The Finnish Experience in the Western Great Lakes Region: New Perspectives* (Turku, Finland: Institute for Migration, 1975), p. 57.

8. Ibid., pp. 72–73.

9. Unpublished essay by Hyman Berman, "Educations for Work and Labor Solidarity: The Immigrant Miner and Radicalism on the Mesabi Range" (St. Paul, Minnesota: Immigration Archives, 1963), p. 10.

10. Carl Ross, *The Finn Factor in American Labor, Culture and Society*, intro. by Rudolph Vecoli (New York Mills, Minnesota: Parta Printers, 1977), p. 25.

11. Ibid., p. 29.

12. "Ameliorative Factors in the Suomi Synod-Socialist Movement Conflict" in *The Faith of the Finns: Historical Perspectives in the Finnish Lutheran Church in America*, ed. Ralph J. Jalkanen (Lansing: Michigan State University Press, 1972), pp. 235 and 230.

13. Ross, p. 27.

14. Ross, p. 28.

15. William Warren Sweet, *Revivalism in America: Its Origin, Growth, and Decline* (New York: Scribner's Sons, 1944), pp. xi–xiv.

16. Mikko Juva, "The Finnish Evangelical Lutheran Church," *Faith of the Finns*, ed. Ralph J. Jalkanen, pp.23–17.

17. Ralph J. Jalkanen, "Certain Characteristics of the Faith of the Finns," *Faith of the Finns*, p. 51.

18. Ross, pp. 29–30.

19. Ross, p. 56.

20. Douglas Ollila, Jr., "From Socialism to Industrial Unionism (I.W.W.): Social Factors in the Emergence of Left-Labor Radicalism Among Finnish Workers on the Mesabi Range, 1911–1919," *The Finnish Experience*, p. 156.

21. Berman, p. 18.

22. Michael Gary Karni, "Yhteishyva—or, For the Common Good: Finnish Radicalism in the Western Great Lakes Region, 1900–1940." University of Minnesota Dissertation, December 1975, p. 134.

23. Ibid., pp. 136–137.

24. Quoted by Ollila, p. 159.

25. Ibid.

26. Neil Betten, "Riot, Revolution, Repression in the Iron Range Strike of 1916," *Minnesota History* 2, 41 (Summer 1968), p. 82.

27. Ollila, p. 161.

28. Dubofsky, p. 231.

29. Ollila, p. 164.

30. David DeLeon, *The American as Anarchist: Reflections on Indigenous Radicalism* (Baltimore and London: Johns Hopkins University Press, 1978), p. 20.

31. Philip S. Foner, *The International Workers of the World: 1905–1917* (New York: International Publishers, 1965), p. 395f.

32. Sweet, pp. xi–xiv.

33. Betten, p. 86.

34. Dubofsky, p. 324.

35. John Graham Brooks, *American Syndicalism: The I.W.W.* (New York: Macmillan, 1913), pp. 175–176.

36. Foner, pp. 166–167.

37. Betten, p. 89.

38. Ralph Chaplin, *Wobbly: The Rough-and-Tumble Story of an American Radical* (Chicago: University of Chicago Press, 1948), p. 212.

39. Ibid., pp. 211–212.

40. Dubofsky, pp. 158–159.

41. Ollila, "The Suomi Synod as Ethnic Community," in *Faith of the Finns*, p. 260.

42. Karni, p. 77.

7

Conclusion

Walter Rauschenbusch, one of the most important theorists of the Social Gospel movement, proclaimed that "every great movement which . . . profoundly stirs men, unlocks the depths of their religious nature."[1] It is this lofty sentiment that Wobbly Covington Hall seems to be addressing in his article, "Where No Vision Is the People Perish," when he asserts "that all revolutionaries have and must center around some great ideal, some sublime, heart-stirring conception of the world as it ought to be. . . ."[2] Both the Social Gospel preacher and the Wobbly rebel illustrate in these remarks a common note that is central to this study: that is, the prophetic voice—or what Edward Bellamy refers to as "the soul of solidarity."[3]

"There is no denying," writes J. Philip Hyatt in *Prophetic Religion*, "that the prophets were generally more concerned with society as a whole and with social systems and institutions than the individual." Furthermore, Hyatt continues, "they opposed all reliance on vested interests."[4] The elevation of society over the individual is axiomatic to an understanding of Old Testament prophecy, at least until the time of Ezekiel. In his famous 1907 book, *Christianity and the Social Crisis*, Rauschenbusch speaks of the public morality of the prophets as well as their sympathy, "even the most aristocratic among them," with the poor and oppressed classes. It is the prophetic and public side of religion, Rauschenbusch maintains, rather than the private and contemplative, that moves humanity toward action. Of this movement he writes:

When the chaotic mass of humanity stirs to the throb of a new creative day, it always feels the spirit of God hovering over it. The large hope which then beckons men, the ideal of justice and humanity which inspires them, the devotion and self-sacrifice to the cause which they exhibit—these are in truth religious.[5]

Thus, the prophetic message that Rauschenbusch preaches to his flock contains the essential elements of solidarity and social action on behalf of the dispossessed. In his view, these ends can only be achieved by a peaceful alliance between the working class and the middle class—a goal shared by political progressivism. "The ideal society is an organism," Rauschenbusch writes in 1912, "and the Christianizing of the social order must work toward an harmonious cooperation of all individuals for common social ends."[6] This idea, based on the model of Paul's philosophy of the Christian church and the image of Christ-the-Peacemaker, centers on the belief that "the idea of the Kingdom of God must slough off apocalypticism if it is to become the religious property of the modern world."[7]

But the Wobblies, as illustrated throughout this study, take up the banner of class struggle rather than class harmony. They represent a prophetism based on the "apocalypticism" which Rauschenbush warns against. After all, the I.W.W. argues, "even the Nazarene was denounced as a disturber and an enemy of the state and of the established order of things." (*IUB* 1/11/08, p. 3) This remark, originally appearing in the *Nome Industrial Worker*, points toward a characteristic central to Wobbly propheticism. The Christ that appears throughout Wobbly literature and lore is passionately anti-capitalist, anti-state, anti-organized religion and, in short, opposed to any institution that stands in the way of social justice and solidarity.

In dramatic contrast to propheticism is a form of religion that provides the primary target for Wobbly scorn: idolatrous religion. While prophetic religion elevates the virtues of solidarity and social justice, idolatrous religion casts its lot with a set of established institutions or idols. One such institution—

and it is a very powerful one—is the state. In his 1926 essay, "Nationalism as a Religion," Professor Carlton J. H. Hayes of Columbia University draws numerous provocative parallels between modern nationalism and organized religion. He closes the essay with the assertion that "nationalism as a religion inculcates neither charity nor justice, it is proud, not humble; and it signally fails to universalize human aims." As though alluding to a more prophetic form of religion, Professor Hayes continues his assessment of the religion of nationalism by declaring that it "repudiates the revolutionary message of St. Paul and proclaims anew the primitive doctrine that there shall be Jew and Greek, only that now there shall be Jew and Greek more quintessentially than ever." Furthermore, it invariably ushers in "tribal selfishness and vainglory, a particularly ignorant and tyrannical intolerance,—and war."[8]

For the I.W.W., the primary institution of capitalist oppression is the state, "all of whose powers of coercion, direct and indirect, are utilized for its perpetuation. And the ethics, the morals and the religions conform thereto." (*IUB* 2/15/08, p. 3) It was "profit-mongers and the political tyrants" of the state, they argue, who crucified Jesus, the most prominent enemy of the state. But they insist:

By the same token that persecution did not smother the hopes of the "undesirable" Nazarene so also the industrial and political tyrants of the twentieth century fail to move the workers from their ideal, which is the emancipation of humanity and the establishment of real civilization. (*IUB* 4/11/08, p. 3)

Another barrier to the "real civilization" prophesized by the I.W.W., besides the state, is the "idol" of the individual. It is not surprising that literature of the I.W.W. is filled with unkind words for selfish individualism, a quality inherently opposed to labor organization. Likewise, the Social Gospel preachers, almost to a person, condemned excessive individualism as a serious barrier to progress. Rauschenbusch, for example, traces the unfortunate transition of religion from the public faith of the Old Testament prophets to the "personal religion" of later Christianity. "In religious individualism," he writes:

Even in its sweetest forms, there was a subtle twist of self-seeking which vitiated its Christlikeness. Thomas a Kempis', "Imitation of Christ," and Bunyan's "Pilgrim's Progress" are classical expressions of personal religion, the one Roman Catholic and monastic, the other Protestant and Puritan. In both we are thought to seek the highest good of the soul by turning away from the world of men.[9]

Perhaps the most vocal proponent of personal religion during the Progressive Era was the preacher most often reviled by the Wobblies, William A. (Billy) Sunday. Although favoring such reforms as civic clean-up and prohibition, his revivalistic messages were basically pure individualism, insisting that reception of Christ was the only requirement for salvation. If Walter Rauschenbusch was the most prominent spokesperson of the time for prophetic religion, certainly Billy Sunday was the most publicized proponent of idolatrous religion.

In his closing prayer he insists that "every revival that has swept this land has had two characteristics: First it has been a revival of businessmen. . . . Second, a revival of personal work. . . . I want every man and woman in the audience," says Sunday, "every usher, every member of a committee, to do personal work . . . personal work is what counts."[10] As a champion of American individualism, Sunday won the hearts (and donations) of America's business community and of all those who harbored the nostalgic hope that America would return to an older, simpler tradition. If Sunday had lived during the time of Jesus, one Wobbly writer argues, he would certainly not have been a follower of Christ "when Jesus raided the cornfield" but rather "would have been among the respectable of the time" and soundly condemned such an act of direct action. (*IW* 3/8/09, p. 2)

Besides championing the idolatrous religion of personal salvation instead of the prophetic religion of radical solidarity with the oppressed, Sunday is guilty, in the eyes of the Wobblies, of another unforgivable sin. As his remarks above on the characteristics of revivalism illustrate, he ingratiated himself with business. "Did Billy ever have a word of condemnation for the rich thieves who paid him," the Wobbly quoted above asks rhetorically, "or a good word for the wretches whom they robbed?" To the I.W.W., subservience to or worship of wealth is as idolatrous as subservience to the state or to selfish individualism.

In a poem entitled "The God of Gold," Wobbly poet John F. Lemon condemns the idolatry of gold-worship that often clouds the positive values represented by Christ. Assuming the persona of the idolator, Lemon writes, in the fourth stanza:

> Ye rear rich piles to the God who made all,
> Who exacts neither shelter or meat,
> While mothers must vend their virtue
> That shivering babes may eat.
> For mine is the creed of gain that flaunts
> 'Neath the robes of sanctity,
> The rule of gold o'er the Golden Rule
> Of the man of Galilee. (*IUB* 3/21/08, p. 2)

This poem, like other Wobbly attacks on hypocrisy, illustrates a very important element of propheticism: the continuous effort to point out and expose the gulf that exists, in idolatrous religion, between principle and practice. Billy Sunday preaches Christ-likeness while he milks his audiences. The Salvation Army preaches concern for the poor while it supports the arrest of indigent workers. The Y.M.C.A. preaches peace while it celebrates military heroes. Such contradictions, discussed throughout this study, are condemned in a good deal of Wobbly music, cartoons, speeches and journalism. It is an important task of the prophet to expose the false priests who appear in the guise of true religion.

Edward Bellamy, often read by the Wobblies,[11] refers significantly to the difference between the true representatives of God and the false prophets of idolatrous religion. In Chapter 23 of *Equality*, the 1897 sequel to his novel, *Looking Backward*, Bellamy relates "The Parable of the Water Tank" in which the development of capitalism and its abuses is told in scriptural language. Briefly, the parable tells of a dry, parched land where profiteers gain control of the only water supply. "Howbeit," the parable begins, "there were certain men in that land who were more crafty and diligent than the rest, and these had gathered stores of water where others would find none and the name of these men was called capitalists." The capitalists, crafty as they were, soon gained the allegiance of many of the so-called religious leaders. By the end of the parable, however, thanks to the cooperation of "agitators," the "true priests," and the majority of the people, the tyranny of capitalism is overthrown. The parable ends with a triumphant, prophetic note:

> Howbeit, there were certain true priests of the living God who would not prophesy for the capitalists, but had compassion on the people; and when they heard the shouting of the people . . . they rejoiced with exceeding great joy, and gave thanks to God because of the deliverance.[12]

The I.W.W., like Bellamy in his parable, often uses the scriptural mode to criticize capitalism and its various institutions. And, as in Bellamy, this language often serves to point out the gulf that exists between principle and practice in the institutional religions of the world. Most historians of the I.W.W., however, view these passages in the same way that they view the Wobbly songs based on hymn tunes: as mere parody. Although Wobbly writers and composers certainly excel as parodists, burlesquing and imitating traditional, often Christian forms, the religious spirit of the I.W.W. goes beyond parody and into the realm of prophecy. When the I.W.W. parodies, it is not a parody bristling with the utmost contempt for all religion, but one that points an accusing finger at the false prophets who attempt to mislead and exploit the working class in the name of religion.

The songs and cartoons, speeches and poems of the I.W.W. provide a system of beliefs and symbols for the "working stiffs" of the Progressive Era and reveal the prospects for a "commonwealth of toil that is to be." This revelation, central to the definition proposed at the beginning of this study, is always strengthened by the force and hope of prophetic religion. "When labor shall assume its rightful place upon the throne of universal liberty," one writer proclaims, "the chaos of artificial kings and rulers will cease."[13]

But once one gains an understanding of or appreciation for the unique features of the Wobbly faith, as seen in the union's songs, press, poetry, rhetoric and actions, how does one assess the I.W.W.'s significance in a broader, cultural and historical context? Is the union a mere anomaly in American history that teaches us nothing about the labor movement, radicalism or American culture generally?   On the contrary, the lesson of the I.W.W. is a valuable lesson about how religious sensibility and imagery helped mobilize the radical element of the labor movement in a way that guarantees the Wobblies a permanent and important place in American labor lore. If Wobbly Covington Hall is correct when he writes that "Where No Vision is, the People Perish,"[14] then the songs and writings of the I.W.W. provide the rootless workers with a vision and a faith greater than any other movement in pre–World War I America.

Historians such as Robert H. Wiebe sell the I.W.W. short when they characterize the union as offering primarily the threatening "spector of a nationwide league of the unwashed."[15] Perhaps if Mr. Wiebe had studied the union carefully enough to have discovered that it is not called the "International Workers of the World,"[16] he would have realized that the I.W.W. represented much more than unwashed rabble; much more than Daniel De Leon's characterization of them as the "slum proletariat." Such epithets dismiss the possibility of any need for serious investigation of the I.W.W.

Emerging and maturing during the Progressive Era, the I.W.W. provided a revolutionary model for social change in a period that Wiebe correctly sees as dominated by "the ambition of the new middle class to fulfill its destiny through bureaucratic means."[17] To the proponent of progressivism, the interests of the working class as well as the business class must always be subjugated to something called the "general public," which might be characterized simply as the "middle class." It is this class that Theodore Roosevelt champions when he asserts: "I refuse to assent to the view that either the owners of the property, or the workers, have interests paramount to the general interest of the public at large."[18]

To the progressives, both political and religious, the middle class represents a sacred ground where harmony, not struggle, must exist between the workers and the owners. "Just as the Protestant principle of religious liberty and the democratic principle of political liberty rose to victory by an alliance with the middle class," writes Rauschenbusch, "so the new Christian principle of brotherly association must ally itself with the working class if both are to conquer."[19] Such a principle—one might call it a principle of class collaboration—dominated the culture of the Progressive Era.

In the realm of labor, this principle is embodied in the "pure and simple unionism" of Samuel Gompers. Fleeing from the visionary unionism of Terrence Powderly and the Knights of Labor of the 1870's and 1880's, Gompers sought to convince workers of the 1890's and 1900's to avoid the rocky road of struggle in favor of the smooth path of class harmony. But "pure and simple unionism," says one Wobbly writer of 1907, "is based upon harmony and brotherhood of the capitalist class and the working class" and the Progressive Era lesson that "the capitalist is indispensible to the working class; that capital and labor must go hand in hand. . . ."[20]

The inevitable result of such collaboration, says the Wobbly writer, is the appearance of various labor relations boards "in which the fakir official and the leading employers meet together in friendly conclave and decide amicably the extent to which the laborer is to be plundered."[21] In contrast to what the Wobblies saw as the capitalist god of harmony, the Wobblies posited a prophetic Christ who is "a proletaire, a Nazarene, the carpenter; whose words make systems, states and empires turn to dust."[22] If the working class needs a god, says Walker P. Smith let it not be the capitalist God of harmony and collaboration, but a God "of the working class, by the working class, for the working class."[23]

Besides providing a striking contrast to the "search for order" and harmony that characterizes the political, economic and religious rhetoric of the Progressive Era, the I.W.W. offered a vision of the future that was dramatically different from the primarily middle class utopian novels that flourished in America between the 1880's and 1900.[24] Most of these late nineteenth century novels offered the American readers ways of coping with the chaotic changes occurring in an increasingly urbanized and industrialized society. The middle class prophets who wrote these novels, such as Edward Bellamy and Ignatius Donnelly, generally present a vision of class harmony quite compatible with the dream of the Progressive Era. The "revolution" of Bellamy's *Looking Backward*, for example, occurs without a class struggle. This novel, like most of the utopian works of the late nineteenth century, serves as "a sensitive indicator of where the sharpest anguish" of the Progressive Era lies,[25] as well as a "speculative myth" for anticipating the future in a chaotic age.

But while the utopian authors followed in the footsteps of Progressivism, depicting a future of class collaboration and harmony, the I.W.W. raised an angry, prophetic voice of struggle and change, of building "a new world in the shell of the old." Like Christ, the members of the I.W.W. saw their mission "not to send peace but a sword."[26] At a time in history when the utopian novel was in decline, offering little more than a vision of America-as-utopia, the I.W.W. offered a "speculative myth" of the future that was both dynamic and revolutionary. This myth is embodied most profoundly in Father Thomas J. Hagerty's so-called "Wheel of Fortune," an ingenious scheme that divides all wage-earning occupations into eight departments. Unlike the primarily static utopian novels, Hagerty's wheel "will build up within itself the structure of an Industrial Democracy—a Workers' Cooperative Republic—which must finally burst the shell of capitalist government."[27]

And at a time when American Protestantism, by the close of the nineteenth century, was devising a blueprint for world domination by Anglo-Saxon Christianity,[28] the I.W.W. was reviving, in syndicalist, class struggle terms, the revolutionary, system-rattling energy of prophecy; the anti-capitalist fervor of a religion of the dispossessed. One Wobbly writing in a pre-Christmas issue of *Solidarity* states:

The modern militant of the labor movement may without hypocrisy pause to do homage to the humble yet heroic carpenter of Nazareth. Despised as we are despised; hunted as we are hunted—he seems like one of our kind, with whom we may clasp fraternal hands across the centuries and bid to be of good cheer, since his ideal of universal brotherhood based upon toil is not forgotten—and is about to be realized.[29]

Such is the soul of the Wobblies: nurtured by solidarity, rooted in class struggle and vitalized by religious zeal for the working class.

NOTES

1. Walter Rauschenbusch, *Christianity and the Social Crisis*, ed. Robert D. Cross (New York: Harper Torchbook ed., 1964), p. 319.

2. Covington Hall, "Where No Vision Is the People Perish," *Industrial Worker*, August 26, 1909, p. 4.

3. Edward Bellamy, "Religion of Solidarity," *Edward Bellamy: Selected Writings on Religion and Society* (New York: Liberal Arts Press, 1955), pp. 8–9.

4. J. Philip Hyatt, *Prophetic Religion* (New York and Nashville: Abingdon-Cokesbury Press, 1947), p. 74.

5. Rauschenbusch, *Crisis*, pp. 11 and 319.

6. Walter Rauschenbusch, *Christianizing the Social Order* (New York: Macmillan, 1912), pp. 366–367.

7. Ibid., p. 56.

8. Carlton J. H. Hayes, "Nationalism as a Religion," *Essays on Nationalism* (New York: Macmillan, 1926), p. 125.

9. Rauschenbusch, *Christianizing*, pp. 111–112.

10. Gerald N. Brob and Robert N. Beck, eds. *American Ideas: Source Readings in the Intellectual History of the United States*, Vol. 2 (New York: The Free Press, 1963), pp. 206–207.

11. Melvyn Dubofsky, in *We Shall Be All* (New York: Quadrangle Press, 1969), points out that Bellamy was a popular author in I.W.W. bookshelves. (p. 147)

12. Edward Bellamy, *Equality* (New York: Greenwood Press—reprint of D. Appleton and Company's 1897 ed.—1969), pp. 195 and 203.

13. Clinton Simonton, "Be Not Like Dumb, Driven Cattle," *Industrial Union Bulletin*, November 9, 1907, p. 1.

14. *IW*, August 26, 1909, p. 4.

15. Robert H. Wiebe, *Search for Order, 1877–1920* (New York: Hill and Wang, 1966), p. 204.

16. It is thus misnamed twice in Mr. Wiebe's book.

17. Wiebe, p. 166.

18. Theodore Roosevelt, *The Foes of Our Own Household* (New York: George H. Doran Co., 1917), p. 116.

19. Rauschenbusch, *Crisis*, p. 409.

20. "Industrial Unionism," *IUB*, October 12, 1907, p. 3.

21. Ibid.

22. From the poem entitled "The Proletaire" by Stanislaus Cullen, *IW*, July 23, 1910, p. 2.

23. Walker P. Smith, "The God of Our Masters," *IW*, July 2, 1910, p. 3.

24. Kenneth M. Roemer, in his 1976 book, *The Obsolete Necessity: America in Utopian Writings, 1888–1900*, lists 150 titles in the dozen years that he examines.

25. Introduction to Frank E. Manual's *Utopias and Utopian Thought* (Boston: Beacon Press, 1965).

26. Matthew 10:34.

27. From Hagerty's article in the May 1905, issue of the *Voice of Labor*.

28. See Robert T. Handy's *A Christian America: Protestant Hopes and Historical Realities* (London: Oxford University Press, 1971), especially Chapter 5 entitled "The Christian Conquest of the World, 1890–1920."

29. "Birth of Christianity," *Solidarity*, December 23, 1916, p. 2.

Appendix I

The Preamble to the Constitution of the Industrial Workers of the World appeared in the Proceedings of the 1908 I.W.W. Convention in the I.W.W. *Industrial Union Bulletin* (November 7, 1908).

PREAMBLE OF THE INDUSTRIAL WORKERS OF THE WORLD

The working class and the employing class have nothing in common. There can be no peace so long as hunger and want are found among millions of working people and the few, who make up the employing class, have all the good things of life.

Between these two classes a struggle must go on until the workers of the world organize as a class, take possession of the earth and the machinery of production, and abolish the wage system.

We find that the centering of management of the industries into fewer and fewer hands makes the trade unions unable to cope with the ever growing power of the employing class. The trade unions foster a state of affairs which allows one set of workers to be pitted against another set of workers in the same industry, thereby helping defeat one another in wage wars. Moreover, the trade unions aid the employing class to mislead the workers into the belief that the working class have interests in common with their employers.

These conditions can be changed and the interest of the working class upheld only by an organization formed in such a way that all its members in any one industry, or in all industries if necessary, cease work whenever a strike or lockout is on in any department thereof, thus making an injury to one an injury to all.

Instead of the conservative motto, "A fair day's wage for a fair day's work," we must inscribe on our banner the revolutionary watchword, "Abolition of the wage system."

It is the historic mission of the working class to do away with capitalism. The army of production must be organized, not only for the every-day struggle with capitalists, but also to carry on production when capitalism shall have been overthrown. By organizing industrially we are forming the structure of the new society within the shell of the old.

Appendix II

Hold the Fort.

P.P.B.

P.P. Bliss

1. Ho, my com~rades! See the sig~nal Wav~ing in the sky! Re~in~force~ments
2. See the might~y host ad~van~cing, Sa~tan lead~ing on: Might~y men a~

now ap~pear~ing, Vic~to~ry is nigh. "Hold the fort, for I am com~ing,"
round us fall~ing, Cour~age al~most gone.

Chorus.

Je~sus sig~nals still; Wave the answer back to heav~en, "By Thy grace we will."

Onward, Christian Soldiers.
Sabine Gould.
Arthur Sullivan.
On-ward Christian soldiers! Marching as to war, With the cross of Je-sus
At the sign of tri-umph, Satan's host doth flee; On, then, Christian soldiers,
Go-ing on be-fore; Christ the roy-al Master, Leads a-gainst the foe;
On to vic-to-ry! Hell's foun-da-tions quiv-er At the shout of praise,
Refrain.
For-ward in-to bat-tle, See His ban-ner go!
Broth-ers, lift your voic-es, Loud your anthems raise.
On-ward Christian
sol-diers! Marching as to war, With the cross of Je-sus Going on be-fore.

Thos. Ken.

Praise God.

Rev. George Coles.

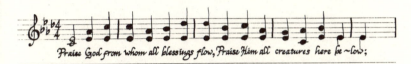

Praise God from whom all blessings flow, Praise Him all creatures here be~low;

Praise Him a~bove ye heav'nly hosts; Praise Father, Son and Ho~ly Ghost.

Praise God from whom all blessings flow, Praise Him all creatures here be~low.

Revive Us Again.

Wm. P. Mackay.   J. J. Husband.

We praise Thee, O God! For the Son of Thy love, For Je~sus who
We praise Thee, O God! For Thy Spir~it of light, Who has shown us our

died, And is now gone a~bove.
Sav~iour, and scat~tered our night:

Refrain.

Hal~le~lu~jah! Thine the glo~ry, Hal~le
~lu~jah! A~men! Hal~le~lu~jah! Thine the glo~ry, Re~vive us a~gain.

Sweet By-and By.

S. Filmore Bennett.   Jos. P. Webster.

1. There's a land that is fair~er than day, And by faith we can see it a~
2. We shall sing on that beau~ti~ful shore The mel~o~di~ous songs of the

far; For the Fa~ther waits o~ver the way, To pre~pare us a
blest, And our spir~its shall sor~row no more, Not a sigh for the

Chorus.

dwell~ing place there. In the sweet   by~and~by,   We shall
bless~ing of rest.

In the sweet   by~and~by,

meet on that beau~ti~ful shore,   In the sweet   by~and~

by~and~by,   by~and~by, by~and~

by,   We shall meet on that beau~ti~ful shore.
by, By~and~by,

There is Power in the Blood.

Rev. E. S. Ufford.

Throw out the Life-Line.

Arr. by Geo. C. Stebbins.

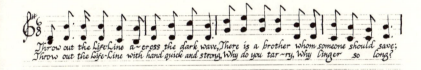

Throw out the Life-Line a~cross the dark wave, There is a brother whom someone should save;
Throw out the Life-Line with hand quick and strong, Why do you tar~ry, Why linger so long?

Somebod~y's brother! oh, who then, will dare To throw out the Life-Line his per~il to share?
See he is sinking; oh, hast~en to~day—And out with the Life-Boat! away, then, a~way!

Chorus.

Throw out the Life-Line! Throw out the Life-Line! Some one is drift~ing a~way;

Throw out the Life-Line! Throw out the Life-Line! Some one is sink~ing to~day.

Bibliography

Ahlstrom, Sidney E. *A Religious History of the American People*. New Haven and London: Yale University Press, 1972.

Ashleigh, Charles. "The Poetry of Revolt." *The Little Review*, 1, No. 6 (September 1914), 22–25.

Banton, Michael, ed. *Anthropological Approaches to the Study of Religion*. New York: Frederick A. Praeger Publishers, 1966.

Beer, Max. *Fifty Years of International Socialism*. New York: Macmillan, 1935.

———. *Social Struggles and Socialist Forerunners*. New York: International Publishers, 1929.

Bellamy, Edward. *Equality*. D. Appleton and Company, 1897; rpt. New York: Greenwood Press, 1969.

———. *Selected Writings on Religion and Society*. Ed. and introd. Joseph Schiffman. New York: The Liberal Arts Press, 1955.

Berman, Hyman. "Education for Work and Labor Solidarity: The Immigrant Miners and Radicalism on the Mesabi Range." St. Paul, Minnesota: Immigration Archives, 1963.

Betten, Neil. "Riot, Revolution, Repression in the Iron Range Strike of 1916." *Minnesota History*, 41, No. 2 (Summer 1968), 82–93.

Brazier, Richard. "The Story of the I.W.W.'s 'Little Red Songbook.' " *Labor History*, 2, No. 1 (Winter 1968), 91–104.

Brissenden, Paul Frederick. *The I.W.W.: A Study of American Syndicalism*. New York: Columbia University, 1920.

Bronowski, J. *William Blake and the Age of Revolution*. New York: Harper and Row, 1965.

Brooks, John Graham. *American Syndicalism: The I.W.W.* New York: Macmillan, 1913.

————. *Labor's Challenge to the Social Order: Democracy Its Own Critic and Educator*. New York: Macmillan, 1920.

Brown, D. Mackenzie. *Ultimate Concern: Tillich in Dialogue*. New York: Harper and Row, 1965.

Calmer, Alan. "The Wobbly in American Literature." *New Masses*, (18 September 1934), 21.

Cannon, James P. *The I.W.W.* New York: Merit Publishers, 1955.

Chaplin, Ralph. *Bars and Shadows: The Prison Poems of Ralph Chaplin*. New York: The Leonard Press, 1927.

————. *Wobbly: The Rough-and-Tumble Story of an American Radical*. Chicago: University of Chicago Press, 1948.

Clark, S. D. *Church and Sect in Canada*. Toronto: University of Toronto Press, 1948.

Coleman, McAliston. *Eugene V. Debs: A Man Unafraid*. New York: Greenberg Publishers, 1930.

Conlin, Joseph R., ed. *The American Radical Press, 1880–1960*. Vol. I. Westport, Connecticut: Greenwood Press, 1974.

Cuddihy, John Murray. *No Offense: Civil Religion and Protestant Taste*. New York: Seabury Press, 1978.

Curwen, John Spencer. *Studies in Worship Music*. 2nd Series. London: J. Curwen and Sons, 1885.

Debs, Eugene V. "Hagerty on the Hustings." *American Labor Journal*. 29 January 1903, 6.

————. *His Life, Writings and Speeches (Authorized)*. St. Louis: Phil Wagner, 1908.

————. "The Socialist Party's Appeal." *The Comrade*, 3, No. 5 (October 1904), 291–292.

DeCaux, Len. *The Living Spirit of the Wobblies*. New York: International Publishers, 1978.

De Leon, Daniel. *Preamble of the Industrial Workers of the World*. New York: Socialist Labor Party Press, 1914.

Denisoff, R. Serge. *Great Day Coming: Folk Music and the American Left*. Urbana, Illinois: University of Illinois Press, 1971.

————. *Sing a Song of Social Significance*. Ohio: Bowling Green University Popular Press, 1972.

————, and Richard A. Peterson. *The Sounds of Social Change*. Chicago: Rand, McNally and Co., 1972.

Dinnerstein, Leonard, and Kenneth T. Jackson, eds. *American Vistas: 1877 to the Present*. New York: Oxford University Press, 1971.

Doherty, Robert E. "Thomas J. Hagerty, the Church, and Socialism." *Labor History*, 3, No. 1 (Winter 1962), 39–56.

Douglas, Mary, and Steven Tipton, eds. *Religion and America: Spiritual Life in a Secular Age*. Boston: Beacon Press, 1982.

Dowell, Eldridge Foster. *A History of Criminal Syndicalism in the United States*. Baltimore: Johns Hopkins Press, 1939.

Dubofsky, Melvyn. *We Shall Be All: A History of the I.W.W.* New York: Quadrangle, 1969.

Durkheim, Emile. *The Elementary Forms of the Religious Life*. Trans. Joseph Ward Swain. New York: Collier, 1961.

Eliot, Charles W. *The Conflict Between Individualism and Collectivism in a Democracy*. New York: Charles Scribner's Sons, 1910.

Flynn, Elizabeth Gurley. *The Rebel Girl: An Autobiography*. New York: International Publishers, 1955.

Foner, Philip S. *The Case of Joe Hill*. New York: International Publishers, 1965.

———. *The Industrial Workers of the World, 1905–1917*. Vol. 4 of *History of the Labor Movement in the United States*. New York: International Publishers, 1965.

———. *The Letters of Joe Hill*. New York: Oak Publications, 1965.

The Founding Convention Notes of the I.W.W.: Proceedings. 1905; rpt. New York: Merit Publishers, 1969.

Gerlach, Luther P., and Virginia H. Hine. *People, Power, Change: Movements of Social Transformation*. Indianapolis and New York: Bobbs-Merrill, 1970.

Gilbert, James. *Designing the Industrial State: The Intellectual Pursuit of Collectivism in America, 1880–1940*. Chicago: Quadrangle Books, 1972.

Ginger, Ray. *The Bending Cross: A Biography of Eugene Victor Debs*. New York: Russell and Russell, 1949.

Giovannitti, Arturo. *Arrows in the Gale*. Intro. by Helen Keller. Riverside, Connecticut: Hillacre Book House, 1914.

———. *The Collected Poems of Arturo Giovannitti*. Intro. by Norman Thomas. Chicago: E. Clemente, 1962.

Glock, Charles Y., and Rodney Stark. *Religion and Society in Tension*. Chicago: Rand McNally and Co., 1965.

Grob, Gerald N., and Robert N. Beck, eds. *American Ideas: Source Readings in the Intellectual History of the United States*. Vol. 2. New York: The Free Press, 1963.

Hagerty, Thomas J. "How I Became a Socialist." *Comrade*, 2, No. 1 (October 1902), 6–7.

Hall, Covington. *Songs of Love and Rebellion*. New Orleans: John J. Weihing Printing Co., 1915.

Hampton, Wayne. "The Politics of Music: A Case Study of the I.W.W." Popular Culture Conference, Pittsburgh. April 1979.

Handy, Robert T. "Christianity and Socialism in America, 1900–1920." *Church History*, 21, No. 1 (March 1952), 39–54.

———. *A Christian America: Protestant Hopes and Historical Realities*. London: Oxford University Press, 1971.

Hayes, Carlton J. H. *Essays on Nationalism*. New York: Macmillan Co., 1926.

Haywood, William D. *Bill Haywood's Book*. New York: International Publishers, 1929; rpt. Westport, Conn.: Greenwood Press, 1983.

Hobsbawm, E. J. *Primitive Rebels: Studies in Archaic Forms of Social Movement in the 19th and 20th Centuries*. Manchester, England: Manchester University Press, 1959.

Hofstadter, Richard. *The Age of Reform: From Bryant to F. D. R.* New York: Alfred Knopf, 1956.

Holloway, Mark. *Heavens on Earth: Utopian Communities in America, 1680–1880*. London: Turnstile Press, 1951.

Hopkins, Charles Howard. *The Rise of the Social Gospel in American Protestantism, 1865–1915*. New Haven, Connecticut: Yale University Press, 1940.

Hyatt, J. Philip. *Prophetic Religion*. New York and Nashville: Abingdon-Cokesbury Press, 1947.

Jalkanen, Ralph J. *The Faith of the Finns: Historical Perspectives on the Finnish Lutheran Church in America*. Lansing, Michigan: Michigan State University Press, 1972.

Johnson, Benton. "On Church and Sect." *American Sociological Review*, 28, No. 4 (August 1963), 539–549.

Johnstone, Ronald L. *Religion and Society in Interaction: The Sociology of Religion*. Englewood Cliffs, New Jersey: Prentice Hall, 1975.

Jones, James. *From Here to Eternity*. New York: Charles Scribner's Sons, 1952.

Karni, Michael G.; Matti E. Kaups; and Douglas Ollila, Jr., eds. *The Finnish Experience in the Western Great Lakes Region*. Turku, Finland: Institute for Migration, 1975.

———. *Yhteishyva—Or, For the Common Good*. University of Minnesota Dissertation, December 1975.

Karsner, David. *Debs: His Authorized Life and Letters*. New York: Boni and Liveright, 1919.

Karson, Marc. *American Labor Unions and Politics, 1900–1918*. Boston: Beacon Press, 1965.

Kay, Ernest, ed. *International Who's Who in Music and Musician's Directory*, 7th ed. Cambridge: University Press, 1975.

Kornbluh, Joyce L., ed. *Rebel Voices: An I.W.W. Anthology*. Ann Arbor: University of Michigan Press, 1964.

Latta, M. C. "The Background for the Social Gospel in American Protestantism." *Church History*, 5 (1936), 256–270.

Link, Arthur S. *Woodrow Wilson and the Progressive Era, 1910–1917*. New York: Harpers, 1954.

Luckman, Thomas. *The Invisible Religion: The Problem of Religion in American Society*. New York: Macmillan, 1967.

MacGowan, Kenneth. "Giovannitti: A Poet of the Wop." *The Forum*, 52 (October 1914), 609–611.

Manuel, Frank E., and P. Fritzie. *Utopian Thought in the Western World*. Cambridge: Belknap Press, 1979.

————, ed. *Utopias and Utopian Thought*. Boston: Beacon, 1965.

Maróthy, János. *Music and the Bourgeois, Music and the Proletarian*. Budapest: Akademiai Kiado, 1974.

Marty, Martin. *Righteous Empire: The Protestant Experience in America*. New York: Dial Press, 1970.

May, Henry F. *The End of Innocence: A Study of the First Years of Our Own Time, 1912–1917*. New York: Alfred A. Knopf, 1959.

————. *Protestant Churches and Industrial America*. New York: Octagon Books, 1963.

McEnroe, Thomas H. "The I.W.W.: Theories, Organizational Problems and Appeals, as Revealed Principally in the Industrial Worker." Dissertation, University of Minnesota, 1960.

Milburn, George. *The Hobo's Hornbook: A Repertory for a Gutter Jongleur*. New York: Ives Washburn, 1930.

Morton, A. L. *The Everlasting Gospel: A Study in the Sources of William Blake*. London: Lawrence and Wisehart, 1958.

Mowry, George E. *The Era of Theodore Roosevelt, 1900–1912*. New York: Harper, 1958.

Newman, William M. *The Social Meaning of Religion*. Chicago: Rand-McNally, 1974.

Niebuhr, H. Richard. *Christ and Culture*. New York: Harper and Row, 1951.

————. *The Social Sources of Denominationalism*. Cleveland and New York: Meridian Books, 1929.

Nolan, Dean, and Fred Thompson. *Joe Hill: I.W.W. Songwriter*. Chicago: Industrial Workers of the World, 1979.

Parker, Carleton H. *The Casual Laborer and Other Essays*. New York: Russell and Russell, 1920.

Parrington, Vernon L. *American Dreams: A Study of American Utopias*. New York: Russell and Russell, 1964.

Pells, Richard H. *Radical Visions and American Dreams: Culture and Social Thought in the Depression Years*. New York: Harper and Row, 1973.

Perlman, Mark. *Labor Union Theories in America: Background and Development*. Evanston, Illinois: Row, Peterson and Co., 1958.

Pfeiffer, C. Whit. "From 'Bohunks' to Finns." *Survey: A Journal of Social Exploration*, 26, No. 1 (1 April 1916), 8–14.

"The Poetry of Syndicalism." *Atlantic Monthly*. June 1913, 853–854.

Pope, Liston. *Millhands and Preachers: A Study of Gastonia*. New Haven and London: Yale University Press, 1942.

Powderly, Terence V. *The Path I Trod*. New York: Columbia University Press, 1940.

Quint, Howard H. *The Forging of American Socialism: Origins of the Modern Movement*. Indianapolis: Bobbs-Merrill, 1953.

Rauschenbusch, Walter. *Christianity and the Social Crisis, 1907*. Ed. Robert D. Cross. New York: Harper Torch Book, 1964.

———. *Christianizing the Social Order*. New York: Macmillan, 1912.

Rayback, Joseph G. *A History of American Labor*. New York: Free Press, 1959.

Renshaw, Patrick. *The Wobblies: The Story of Syndicalism in the United States*. New York: Doubleday and Co., 1967.

Reynolds, William Jensen. *A Survey of Christian Hymnody*. New York: Holt, Rinehart and Winston, 1963.

Richey, Russell E., and Donald G. Jones, eds. *American Civil Religion*. New York: Harper and Row, 1975.

Roemer, Kenneth M. *The Obsolete Necessity: America in Utopian Writings, 1888–1900*. Ohio: Kent State University, 1976.

Roosevelt, Theodore. *The Foes of Our Own Household*. New York: George H. Doran Co., 1917.

Ross, Carl. *The Finn Factor in American Labor, Culture and Society*. New York Mills, Minnesota: Parta Printers, 1977.

Rudich, Norman, ed. *Weapons in Criticism: Marxism in America and the Literary Tradition*. Palo Alto, California: Ramparts Press, 1976.

Sandburg, Carl. *Complete Poems*. New York: Harcourt, Brace and World, 1950.

———. *The Letters of Carl Sandburg*. Ed. Herbert Mitgang. New York: Harcourt, Brace and World, 1968.

———. "The Two Rockefellers and Mr. Walsh." *International Socialist Review*, 16, July 1915, 18–25.

Sandvall, Robert. *The History of the Salvation Army*. 5 vol. London: Thomas Nelson and Sons, 1947–68.

Sankey, Ira. D., et al. *Gospel Hymns: Nos. 1 to 6 Complete*. 1895; rpt. New York: Da Capo Press, 1972.

Saposs, David J. *Left Wing Unionism: A Study of Radical Policies and Tactics*. 1926; rpt. New York: Russell and Russell, 1967.

Simons, A. M. *Class Struggles in America*. Chicago: Charles H. Kerr and Co., 1906.

Sizer, Sandra S. *Gospel Hymns and Social Religion: The Rhetoric of Nineteenth-Century Revivalism*. Philadelphia: Temple University Press, 1978.

Small, Albion W., and George E. Vincent. *An Introduction to the Study of Society*. New York: American Book Co., 1894.

Smith, Gibbs M. *Joe Hill*. Salt Lake City, Utah: University of Utah Press, 1969.

Sorel, Georges. *Reflections on Violence*. Trans. T. E. Hulme. Intro. Edward A. Shils. 1908 1st ed. London: Collier Books, 1950.

Stavis, Barrie, and Frank Harmon, eds. *Songs of Joe Hill*. 1955; rpt. New York: Oak Publications, 1960.

Stedman, Murray S., Jr. *Religion and Politics in America*. New York: Harcourt, Brace and World, 1964.

Stegner, Wallace. *The Preacher and the Slave*. Boston: Houghton Mifflin Co., 1950.

Stevens, Robert M. *Patterns of Protestant Church Music*. Durham, North Carolina: Duke University Press, 1953.

Strout, Cushing. *The New Heavens and New Earth: Political Religion in America*. New York: Harper and Row, 1974.

Sweet, William Warren. *Revivalism in America: Its Origin, Growth, and Decline*. New York: Harper and Row, 1974.

Symes, Lillian, and Travers Clement. *Rebel America: The Story of Social Revolt in the United States*. Boston: Beacon Press, 1972.

Thompson, Fred. *Joe Hill*. San Diego: Fanshen Printing Collective, 1971.

———, and Patrick Murfin. *The I.W.W.: Its First Seventy Years*. Chicago: Industrial Workers of the World, 1976.

Tillich, Paul. *Political Expectation*. New York: Harper and Row, 1971.

"Voices of the Living Poets." *Current Opinion*, 57 July-December 1914, 54.

Weisberger, Bernard A. "Here Comes the Wobblies." *American Vistas: 1877 to the Present*. Eds. Leonard Dinnerstein and Kenneth T. Jackson. New York: Oxford University Press, 1971.

Weyl, Walter. "The Lawrence Strike from Various Angles." *Survey*, 28, No. 1 (1912), pp. 65–80.

Wiebe, Robert H. *The Search for Order: 1877–1920*. New York: Hill and Wang, 1967.

Wilder, Amos N. *The Spiritual Aspects of the New Poetry*. New York: Harper and Brothers Publishers, 1940.

Williams, J. Paul. "The Nature of Religion." *Journal for the Scientific Study of Religion*, 2, No. 1 (October 1962).

Wilson, Woodrow. *The Papers of Woodrow Wilson*. Ed. Arthur S. Link. Princeton, New Jersey: Princeton University Press, 1978.

Yinger, Milton. "Contraculture and Subculture." *American Sociological Review*. (October 1960), 625–635.

Young, Art. *Art Young: His Life and Times*. Ed. John Nicholas Beffel. New York: Sheridan Books, 1939.

Youst, Lionel. "The Wobblies: Solidarity Forever." *North Country Anvil*, 13 (Oct.-Nov. 1974), 12–18.

Index

About the Author

DONALD E. WINTERS, JR., is a faculty member in Humanities at Minneapolis Community College where he teaches in the College for Working Adults.